WORD
BIBLICAL
THEMES

General Editor
David A. Hubbard

Old Testament Editor
John D. W. Watts

New Testament Editor
Ralph P. Martin

WORD
BIBLICAL
THEMES

Isaiah

JOHN D. W. WATTS

WORD PUBLISHING
Dallas · London · Sydney · Singapore

ISAIAH

Word Biblical Themes

Quotations from the Scriptures in this volume are the author's own translation unless otherwise indicated.

Library of Congress Cataloging-in-Publication Data

Watts, John D.W.
    Isaiah / John D.W. Watts.
       p.   cm. — (Word Biblical themes)
    Bibliography: p.
    Includes index.

    1. Bible. O.T. Isaiah—Theology.   2. Bible. O.T. Isaiah—
Criticism, interpretation, etc. I. Title. II. Series.
BS1515.2.W38   1989
224'.106—dc19   89-30790
                                                     CIP

       ISBN 0-8499-0669-5

9 8 0 1 2 3 9 RRD 9 8 7 6 5 4 3 2 1

Printed in the United States of America

To Reid

בני בכורי

CONTENTS

FOREWORD

The Book of Isaiah is the Mount Rushmore of biblical prophecy. Sculpted on its massive slopes are the major themes of Scripture: who God is, what he has done for his people, and how he expects us to serve him. Side by side with these themes stand the figures of the key players in the drama of Israel's life: the prophet himself, the sons of David who ruled Judah from Uzziah to Zerrubabel, and Cyrus, the pagan Persian whom God sovereignly commandeered for sacred service.

No other part of the Bible gives us so panoramic a view of God's handiwork in Israel's history nor such clear perspectives of his lordship over the nations. If Beethoven's nine symphonies loom as landmarks on the horizon of classical music, Isaiah's sixty-six chapters mark the apex of prophetic vision. Their music, their majesty, their mystery combine to inspire, challenge, and intimidate the saints of God from the least to the greatest, from the most naive to the most profound. No other part of Scripture will be well understood without help from the text of Isaiah. John Watts's innovative and sensitive treatment of the prophetic themes is a gift to all who treasure the Bible's truth and aim to live by it.

Word Biblical Themes, a companion series to the Word Biblical Commentary (WBC), seeks to distill the theological essence of the biblical books as interpreted in the more technical series and serve it up in ways that will enrich the preaching, teaching, worship, and discipleship of God's people. Professor Watts, as Old Testament editor of both series, is admirably qualified to make an early contribution to the Themes. His two-volume work on Isaiah in the WBC has set high standards and has been warmly welcomed by scholars, pastors, and students alike.

This exposition of the settings and teachings of Isaiah is sent forth in the hope that it will contribute to the vitality of God's people, renewed by the Word and the Spirit and ever in need of renewal.

Fuller Theological
 Seminary
Pasadena, California

David A. Hubbard
General Editor
Word Biblical Themes
Word Biblical Commentary

PREFACE

Yahweh and his servants

The Book of Isaiah is one of the greatest in the Bible in two respects. On the one hand, its presentation of the character and work of God is revelation at its best. On the other, it treats the theme of serving God and those who do it as comprehensively as any part of Scripture. The main themes of this book fall into these two categories.

The treatment of knowing God uses the names that are applied to him most frequently. These names in turn fall into two categories: God in his governance of the world, the nations, and Canaan, and God as he is known and worshiped in his temple.

The service of God may also be divided into two basic forms that correspond to the understanding of God's work and presence. There are servants of God who relate to him in governing, and there are servants who are related in worship. Again the treatment in this book deals with them accordingly.

Before each of the sections a group of pertinent themes that are basic to Isaiah's presentation are treated. References in the text that follows which refer to the companion volumes in the Word Biblical Commentary are abbreviated as WBC, with volume 24 referring to *Isaiah 1–33* and volume 25 referring to *Isaiah 34–66*.

PART 1
KNOWING GOD AND HIS WAYS

1   KNOWING GOD

The Vision of Isaiah begins with God's complaint that Israel, his own people, his children, had rebelled against him (1:2). He had done so much for them and given them so much, but they did not *know* him. They did not *understand* (1:3).

This theme is central to the book. Israel failed or was unwilling to recognize what God had done and was currently doing for and with them. This unwillingness was rebellion against God's revelation, his leading, and his calling. They preferred to think of God as passive, not stirring until they summoned him. They preferred to seek knowledge and understanding of themselves and their situation or their fate on their own or by pagan astrology, magic, or idolatry. In fact God had shown himself to their fathers through his own initiative. He sought them out. He called. He revealed himself. Their proper role lay in responding to him, in seeing his work, hearing his word, in paying attention to his call. By turning to him, knowledge and understanding were available. Nonetheless this they were unwilling or unable to do. Even after the exile and its judgment on the kingdoms of Israel and Judah for their

3   *Knowing God*

refusal to recognize God in their history, their lives, or their future, most of them continued in the same way—and often, so do we. The condemnation and admonition of the Vision of Isaiah applies to us as well.

Isaiah takes up the basic problem that was identified in Genesis when Adam and Eve could not let alone the Tree of the Knowledge of Good and Evil. Knowledge is necessary in both cases, but there is a right form and a wrong form. Isa 1:18–19 pleads with Israel to be ready to discuss the issue with God: "Come now! Let us test each other . . . become willing and obey." Like Genesis 3, any other course is understood to be rebellious refusal and punished accordingly.

The Vision assumes and proclaims God's revelation of his intention and his interpretation of his acts. It calls on God's people to see God at work, to hear and pay attention to God's instruction, to know and understand what he is doing and saying. We are called to repent, to turn to God so that God can turn to us and make events turn in our favor. We are challenged to "be willing," to "test God" (KJV, "reason together"), and to "wait" on him in hope.

In 6:9–10 the issue of understanding is addressed again. The prophet is told that the time for gaining understanding is passed, and he is given to understand how this should have been achieved. The heart (mind) must be sensitive and receptive. Then people can "see with their eyes" and "hear with their ears." Then they can "turn and have healing." Godly knowledge and understanding is gained in that way. But Israel has refused to do that. Judgment is decreed on the Northern Kingdom in the eighth century B.C. She will not be allowed to repent at that stage. Yet the book will go on to offer new opportunities to the post-Exilic community for this knowledge and understanding.

One of the gifts that God bestows on the king (11:2) is a spirit of understanding and knowledge. So that which God had sought in vain from his people is given freely to the Davidic king so that he can fulfill his function properly (WBC 24:172).

One of the ideal conditions that will characterize the achievement of God's society on earth is that the "knowledge of Yahweh shall cover the land as waters cover the sea" (11:9). How central and how important this knowledge of God is (WBC 24:173).

Israel does not improve. Israel "is not a discerning people," but continues to be blind and deaf to God and his calling (27:11). But a day is coming when the deaf will hear and when the blind will see, when "those errant of spirit will know understanding" (29:22-24). In this time it will be clear that the one "who does not understand" is an idolater.

30:12-18 provides an illustration of what being "rebellious sons, not willing to heed Yahweh's instruction" (30:9) leads to. "Rejecting this word" (30:12), they refuse to go along with God's plan. They will not accept a passive role in world politics as God has called on them to do since the days of Uzziah, so that they can assume a new role as God's spiritual representatives to the world. This calls for a willingness on their part to turn inward in faith and to rest on God's grace and promises.

> In returning and rest you could be saved.
> In quietness and in trust
>   could your heroism consist.
> But you are not willing! (30:15; cf. WBC 24:397)

32:1-8 provides an illustration of what it would be like if "a king should reign in righteousness and . . . princes should rule with justice" (32:1). If the world were turned on its head so values would be right, "if the eyes of those who see should look, and the ears of those who hear should hearken and the mind of the hurried have sense to know" (32:3-4a), then things would be right. The fool would be recognized for what he is (32:5-6), and the noble person would act nobly (32:8). The people of God are still often blind and unperceptive about the ways of God and consequently do not perceive clearly the false ways of leaders in government. When we are

5

blind and irresponsible, we stand judged along with the fools and knaves whom we fail to identify and remove (WBC 24:413–14).

In 37:20, Hezekiah concludes his prayer for deliverance from Sennacherib's siege of Jerusalem with the words:

> Now, Yahweh, our God,
> deliver us from his hand,
> and all the kingdoms of the land shall know
> that you are Yahweh, you alone. (37:20)

Hezekiah pleads with God to see and react to what he sees (37:17), although Hezekiah himself has often rejected God's plan; in fact this very opposition to God's policies announced to his father (chaps. 7–9) was responsible for his present predicament.

Nevertheless, Israel understood God's great acts of salvation (like the Exodus) as a prime means of revelation. So she now prays for deliverance that can be a new means of revelation to all the neighboring peoples (WBC 25:37). 41:20 reads:

> In order that they may see and know,
> that they may position themselves and understand
> (these) together
> that Yahweh's hand has done this
> and that the Holy One of Israel has created it.

This comes at the end of two chapters in which God has announced that good news is coming to Jerusalem and in which he calls on Jewish exiles to carry it to them. Israel complains of human frailty (40:6–7) and of divine neglect (40:27). Then God urges Israel to recognize that all the great things that are happening in her day have been designed by God to serve her interests. If this leaves Israel "poor and needy," it is because she does not need power or wealth to fulfill her role. Cyrus will take care of those things. She is called to worship, rejoice, and sing praises to God. *He will take care of her other needs.*

The New Testament stresses a similar theme for Christians. Paul says "God's power is made perfect in weakness" (2 Cor 12:9, NIV). Heb 13:14 points beyond the privations of this world to "the enduring city," and 1 Pet 1:8 (NIV) calls on believers to be "filled with inexpressible and glorious joy."

Isaiah notes that Israel still needs urging in this respect. God does just that in 49:22-23, calling on Jerusalem in verse 23 to recognize his plan working out in history:

> And you will know that I am Yahweh,
> I in whom those waiting will never be disappointed.

He then assures her of universal recognition:

> And all flesh will know
> that I am Yahweh,
> your Savior and your redeemer,
> Mighty One of Jacob! (49:26b)

A single leader (possibly Zerubabbel; WBC 24:197-98) confesses to being tutored to be what Israel clearly had never learned to be, not rebellious:

> My Lord Yahweh has assigned me a student's tongue
> to know how to sustain a weary one (with) a word.
> He wakes up morning by morning—
>   he wakes up my ear
>   to listen as students do.
> My Lord Yahweh has opened my ear.
> And I, on my part, have not been rebellious.
> I have not turned my back (to him). (50:4-5)

The people continue to "forget" God (51:13), but God continues to reveal himself and hopes the people may know him.

My people shall know my name
in that day
because I am the one who keeps saying "Behold me!"
(52:6)

The great servant passage (52:12-15) announces astonish-ing success and ends with the assurance: "And that of which they had heard nothing they understand" (52:15b). At this point in the book God's plan should be clear and under-standable for all to see. He is working out a way for Israel and Jerusalem through the Persians: first Cyrus and now Darius.

The great chapter 53 is a very complicated passage dealing with understanding. One has died, despised and rejected (53:3), but the recognition comes that "he died for our trans-gressions" (53:4-5a). Furthermore, we understand that heal-ing and wholeness have come to us because of his suffering and death (53:5b-6). That God can actually bring about such healing and effect good through what is a wrongful punish-ment and death is a mystery. Yet we all know of instances in which something like this happens. The New Testament points us to the unique moment when a cross was lifted be-tween heaven and earth with that result.

But such a climax does not make all blindness or rebellion disappear in Israel, or in the church. Isa 56:10 complains:

His watchmen are blind.
None of them knows anything.

Revelation 1-3 also portrays the churches of Asia having lost their eager faith and love.

The frustration of trying to please God is pictured in 58:2 as they are apprised of their rebellions.

Even as they seek me day by day
and delight to know my ways.

Just "meaning well" does not please God. The required knowledge must include an understanding of God's will and his requirements.

The people are devout in their fasting and self-denial (58:3b). But this turns to "strife and contention," even to violence (52:4a). They are told:

You may not fast as (you have) today
(if you want) to make your voice heard on high! (58:4b)

The worship God chooses is:

Opening the bonds of wickedness,
undoing the bindings of a yoke,
and sending out the oppressed to be free. (58:6)

At this stage Israel is still learning the lessons it had desperately needed in chapter 1 on how to worship, and we are still learning them, too.

A generation is condemned in chapter 59 because of wickedness.

They have not known a way of peace
and there is no justice in their paths. (59:8a)

But the promise is renewed to the new generation in Jerusalem that God will now act on their behalf:

you will know that I am Yahweh,
your Savior and your Redeemer,
the Mighty One of Jacob. (60:16b)

As the book moves toward the climactic moment when a new Jerusalem, a new creation, is revealed when all may come to worship, there are still those who want nothing to do with it. God says:

I spread out my hand all day
    toward a rebellious people
    who are walking in ways that are not good,
    after their own thoughts. (65:2)

These are "forsaking Yahweh and forgetting the mount of his holiness" (65:11).

The last great scene has one verse on knowledge even for that day when faith becomes sight:

And you will see and your heart shall rejoice. . . .
And it is known
    that Yahweh's hand (is) with his servants
    and indignation (is) with his enemies. (66:14)

The Book of Isaiah portrays the need to know God, what he is doing, and what he wants. It is very realistic in recognizing that most of us do not want to know, or in knowing, refuse to accept the knowledge as our guide. Yet knowing and obeying means life; refusing and rejecting means death.

Between the golden moments

Biblical history records a few, short, golden moments such as the life of Abraham, the Exodus from Egypt, the year at Sinai, the renewal of the Covenant and the occupation of Canaan (Deuteronomy-Joshua), David and Solomon's reigns, and the restoration of Jerusalem (Ezra-Nehemiah). Between these are long, drab periods like Jacob and his sons in Egypt (four hundred years), the two-hundred-year period of the Judges (Judges-1 Samuel), the divided monarchy to the Exile (ca. four hundred years). Obviously, biblical life is much more occupied with life in the valleys of experience than with moments on its mountaintops. Life and history are still experienced in such terms.

Isaiah depicts a long history of one of these drab periods when the lighter, better moments are relatively few and not very significant. It highlights and celebrates some of those that are surprising: the survival of Jerusalem's royal house and throne in 733 B.C. and 720 B.C. (chaps. 7–9) and (chap. 11), the survival of Jerusalem in 701 B.C. (chaps. 36–39), the return of Sheshbazzar's small expedition and of Zerubbabel's efforts to rebuild the temple in 538 and 518 B.C., and Ezra-Nehemiah's work in 468 and 443 B.C. There is nothing here to compare with the Exodus or the united monarchy, but drab periods can be the showcases for heroism of a peculiar sort and of grace that is noteworthy. Twelve generations of Israelites and Judeans experienced that kind of grace, but they often failed to note the smaller heroic moments that Isaiah depicts. Readers of the book are shown the overarching strategy of God that shaped those centuries, and they can rejoice in the persistent grace and providence that stood watch over an unseeing, unhearing, unknowing, and nonunderstanding people. God's promise and purpose continued to be valid for his people if they would only hear, see, believe, and obey.

Unchanging promises

What are those unchanging promises? What are the forms that have to change from age to age?

Israel had lived with some fixed ideas concerning God's commitments and, therefore, of her fate/future. From Abraham came the firm promise of being a numerous people and of occupying the land of Canaan. From Sinai came a covenant with twelve tribes that they were the heirs of Abraham and would live under God's laws in God's land, enjoying his presence and blessing. From David came the first full control of the promised land and its blessings as well as the promise of an abiding throne in Jerusalem. All of these were fulfilled to varying degrees during the period between the Exodus and the Exile, but they were also for the most part lost during the painful centuries depicted in Isaiah 1–39. The divided Northern Kingdom became an Assyrian province in 731 B.C. After a century and a half of abject vassalage, Judah and Jerusalem were devastated by the Babylonians in 586 B.C., and the king was murdered, although a relative survived in Babylon without country or throne.

Israel's prophets record these devastations. They insist that the Lord, Israel's God, had deliberately brought them about because the people and the kings had broken covenant with him. They were no longer capable of being his people and accomplishing his purpose.

Things needed to be changed, and offending persons, groups, and institutions had to be removed. At the same time, there were numerous questions facing those who survived these calamities. How could God do this and still remain true to his promises to David to give him an heir on his throne in Jerusalem forever? What would happen to God's promise to Abraham to give him a land and a "seed" forever? These seemed to promise that Israel's existence as a people, a nation under a Davidic king, was guaranteed in Canaan forever.

Other questions turned on how the provisions of the Sinai Covenant applied to the situation. The Book of Deuteronomy and the Prophet Jeremiah approached Israel's problem from this direction, seeing a context for understanding the disaster as punishment for breech of covenant but also opening the door to covenant renewal beyond the judgment.

The Vision of Isaiah (like the other prophetic books) tackles these questions head on. It first establishes God's provenance on a broader base, more like that relating to Noah and his sons (Genesis 6–10) as well as his Creator-lordship over all nature. On the understanding that he is Lord of all history and all the nations, he summons first Assyria and then Persia to assume imperial control of the government over all the land (Canaan) as well as a wider frame of empire that encompassed the known world. Thus the economic and political network of tribes and city-states (like that described in Genesis 10), which had in varying forms and degrees been the way of life in the Middle East for over a millennium, was brought to an end. A new age of empire was begun.

It is in this sense that the Assyrian is summoned into Canaan (chaps. 8-10) and the Persian is given Babylon's empire (chaps. 45-47). God has now fashioned a new frame of reference, but what shape would the fulfillment of his purpose and promises take? Obviously they could no longer be the same as they had been before. The new setting also allowed for some accomplishments that the older order did not. The promise to Abraham had spoken of a blessing through Abraham for all the clans of the earth (Gen 12:3). Even David's wider scope of authority only reached the nations of "the land" (Psalm 2), that is, of Canaan. David's reign also was promised a wider reach and influence than the land of Canaan and the politics of that age could accommodate.

So while the change to imperial age brought an end to the geographical identity of the twelve tribes in Canaan and the political identity with Israel's own king in Jerusalem, it also opened new possibilities for living out and experiencing the gracious purpose of God in Israel's existence as a people. The prophets opened doors to the faith, the hope, and even the understanding that related to these. The Book of Isaiah draws its own particular picture of that future with God.

First, they said, things are not always what they seem. Knowledge and understanding require that one keep up with God's goals, decisions, and strategies if one is to evaluate events and their significance. Isaiah contends that Israel's troubles in the eighth century were due to her own apostasy, the working out of rebellion that began with the division of the kingdom; that the Assyrian's invasions were not simply the work of a greedy, violent neighbor, but were the intended work of God himself; that Ahaz's policies of appeasement were not simply the traitorous and cowardly policies of a weak and idolatrous king, but were in obedience to the revealed purposes of God with the Assyrian; that Hezekiah's rebellions were not the courageous and principled work of a hero, but the unwise and willful sin of a rebel against God's announced strategy for Judah that almost lost him his capitol and his throne a century before it had to be.

Isaiah further sees the Persian emperors, Cyrus (explicitly) and Darius and Artaxerxes (implicitly) not as rapacious conquerors, but as servants of God who will build his temple in Jerusalem. This list could be extended. Seen from God's perspective, things are often different than one usually judges them to be.

Second, the prophet said that the divine promises are still valid. God's strategy still has a vital role for Israel in this new and very different age. This new role is even furthered by Israel's condition: being scattered through the empire. A number of the older forms of fulfillment, however, are not mentioned, the twelve tribes in Canaan and the Davidic kingship being two that are omitted.

The new shape of promise-fulfillment in Isaiah revolves around worship in a rebuilt Jerusalem and on Israel continuing to be recognized as God's Servant (parallel to Cyrus), even in Babylon. God's purpose is furthered by a servant-leadership in Jerusalem, even when that involves submission to abuse (chap. 50) and death (chap. 53). The Vision takes up aspects of Abraham's promise and David's role that have not usually been stressed; Israel's new servant role is to highlight these.

Pride and humility

God's problems with mankind have turned on the human tendency toward arrogant pride and ambition. Genesis makes this plain in the stories about Adam, Eve, and Cain (chaps. 3–4) and the tower of Babel (11:1–9). Isaiah picks up the theme and reemphasizes that such haughty pride is ultimately intolerable to God.

There is a day belonging to Yahweh of Hosts
   upon everything high and raised
and upon everything lifted up—and it shall fall. . . .
And the haughtiness of the human shall be brought down
   and the exaltation of men shall be abased

and Yahweh alone shall be exalted
   in that day. (2:12, 17; see WBC 24:37)

Politically, the fall of Babylon is portrayed as the symbol of
every tyrant's fate:

"How oppressing has ceased!
Arrogance has ceased!
Yahweh has shattered
the staff of the evil ones,
the rod of rulers. . . .
All the land is at rest, is quiet.
They break into joyful song."
(14:4b–5, 7; WBC 24:204)

Israel's rebellion against God and God's strategy is, at
least in part, motivated by this primeval passion. She, too,
wanted to be a nation like the nations (1 Sam 8:20). This
was granted to her with the result that she shared their
fate. The post-Exilic community continued to show signs
of these ambitions, and idolatry and paganism continually pandered to these passions, despite the lessons of their
history.

Indeed, he has humbled those living in the height,
He makes a lofty city fall,
He makes it fall to earth,
He makes it even touch the dust. (26:5)

The absolute requirement for successful servanthood is
humility. It leads to the "knowledge and understanding"
that Israel lacked. It makes it possible to "see" what God is
about and to "hear" what God is saying. Only then are
obedience and faith possible.

The Prophet Isaiah found it necessary to withdraw from
public life to get this: "I will wait for Yahweh who is hiding
his face from the house of Jacob and I will hope for him"

(8:17). The Vision stresses this in terms of "willingness and obedience":

> If you become willing and shall obey,
>   the good of the land you may eat,
> but if you refuse and shall continue obstinate
>   (by a) sword you may be devoured. (1:19–20)

God assures the individual who is "contrite" and "lowly in spirit" that his reviving presence will be with him or her (57:15). He evokes from his listening worshipers a form of service that allows each one:

> A day for a human to humble himself. . . .
> Is not this the fast I would choose:
>   opening the bonds of wickedness,
>   undoing the bindings of a yoke,
>   and sending out the oppressed to be free? . . .
> Is it not sharing your bread with the poor,
>   and that you bring homeless poor persons
>   into your house?
> When you see one naked and you cover him,
>   and you do not hide your self from your own flesh,
> then your light will break out like the dawn
>   and your healing will spring up in a hurry. . . .
> Then you may call
>   and Yahweh will answer (58:5a, 6, 7–8a, 9a).

This service is one of the acts of justice and mercy (58:9b–10), and when one:

> honors (the Sabbath) by not doing your own way
>   not seeking your own pleasure
>   or speaking an (idle) word. (58:13c)

Nehemiah's program (Nehemiah 5) aptly fits this description. Jesus' words in Matt 6:5, 23:6; Luke 11:42–43, 20:46 speak to the imperative for humble service and the abomination of pride, especially in its religious expression.

The vision of the ideal*

The Book of Isaiah is a very realistic book in most ways. It recognizes the inevitable religious results of Israel's apostasy and Jerusalem's infidelity. It sees the political effects of the rise of empires with unclouded vision. It sees the only hope of Exilic and post-Exilic Judaism to lie in being a nonpolitical religious community dependent on the patronage of the Persian emperor.

One central dream gives structure to the book. It is parallel to Micah's use of the same passage (4:1-3). In 2:2-4 Isaiah pictures an exalted Zion as a worship center to which people from all nations will come. There they will encounter God, be taught his ways, and learn to walk in his paths. His word and his law will go out from Zion.

This vision of Zion's future and Judaism's future is fulfilled in Isaiah 66 and in the work of Ezra and Nehemiah. Jerusalem was rebuilt. The temple became a functioning worship center for Judaism, and Jews from all over the known world made their way to Jerusalem for its festivals and to learn what it meant to be a Jew. This continued despite several interruptions until A.D. 70 when Jerusalem was attacked and the temple finally destroyed.

There is also a picture of a child to be born to the House of David in 7:14. Ahaz does have such a child. The fulfillment of that prophecy is hailed in 9:6-7 with all the extravagant royal language that only a monarchy based on divine promises to David and the psalmic ideals of Psalm 2 and others could muster. Ahaz's throne is secure. Hezekiah does succeed him in it. 10:28-34 pictures Yahweh's approach to defend his city. 11:1-5 pictures God's gift of his Spirit to make the new monarch capable of reigning in the style and

*Used by permission, The Theological Educator 35 (1987): 84-90.

fashion of his ancestor, David. 11:10-16 pictures the political goals that needed to be accomplished by a Hezekiah faced with the power of Assyria and with the dispersal of so many from Israel in that time. Some of them had been taken into exile; others had fled the terror at home. A real king would need to restore Israel's capacity to function as a nation and to accept all those voluntary and involuntary exiles back to their homes.

The Book of Isaiah is realistic again in recognizing that Hezekiah, following his own dreams of power, came to his day of helplessness (chaps. 21 and 36-39).

In this period the Book of Isaiah records a vision of what could be in international relations (chap. 19). Israel could play a crucial role in creating a peaceful coexistence with Assyria and Egypt. But again the book is realistic in recognizing that this did not come to pass. The role of Egypt and Assyria in chapters 28-33 confirms the grim picture of reality.

After the fall of Jerusalem and the beginning of the exile, Israel and the broken remnants of Jerusalem are given a vision of restoration in terms that are powerful (chaps. 40-44). Yahweh will raise up a new emperor with the assigned task of restoring Jerusalem. Chapters 45-48 show this to be fulfilled in the rise of Cyrus and the policies of religious tolerance that he effected. However, Jerusalem's actual restoration would come under his successors, Darius who supported Zerubbabel's work (chaps. 49-54) and Artaxerxes who commissioned Ezra and Nehemiah (chaps. 59-66).

This shows that much of the great idealistic vision in Isaiah was directly tied to hopes for Israel's political and religious future. These optimistic pictures were sometimes superseded by the realistic recognition of failures (as in Hezekiah and in Egypt) or by realistic success (as in the post-Exilic restoration of the temple with Persian support).

Radical ideals. But beyond and sometimes intermingled with these ideals of temple and Davidic kingship are others that are even more radically ideal. Micah adds a picture of complete peace (4:4) to the passage that it shares with Isa 2:2–4. In it there is a picture of individual freedom and toleration in which "all nations may walk in the name of their gods; we will walk in the name of the Lord our God for ever and ever."

This was preceded in both Micah and Isaiah by a beautiful picture of disarmament and promise that war will be no more. Persia achieved a partial realization of such religious tolerance. But her determination to extend her empire into Greece ruined all hope of peaceful coexistence with her neighbors and eventually led to her downfall.

The overtones of this idyllic vision of peace among peoples continue to haunt the Book of Isaiah. In 11:6–9 the description of an ideal Spirit-endowed king is followed by a pastoral picture of Jerusalem becoming a simple village in which violence has no part. Not only is there none of the military violence that had stalked Jerusalem's history as a national capital, there is no sign of the social violence that brought Yahweh's condemnation in 1:15, 21–23. There is even no tension between nature's traditional predators and the innocent children. It is as though God's vision would take humanity back to conditions like those in Eden. The Bible pictures no such existence among humans since Adam and Eve were expelled from Eden. Cain and Abel began a reign of violence that had continued unbroken to that time and that continues down to our own time. But the Book of Isaiah insistently inserts a reminder that this violence can in no way be correlated with what God intended. Alongside the revelation of how God works in the midst of this violent and rebellious world, dealing out retribution on its own terms and working out ways to make it possible for his own to worship him, there persists this reminder of the ideal which God intended in creation and still wants for it.

The picture is resumed in 65:17–25. The final verse picks up the themes of 11:6–9, including the refrain, "They will neither harm nor destroy in all my holy mountain." But this is preceded by the announcement of a totally new creation.

That is what it would take to gain this kind of society. The Bible does not picture God turning back the clock of time or the causality of decisions and deeds. It does remind its readers of God's creative power and that none of the world's violence is his idea or the result of his essential will.

This passage relates the ideal to Jerusalem's needs and dreams. God relates to these. He certainly cannot "rejoice" in the realistic picture of Jerusalem in that period or since. He pictures a totally new creation in which he can "rejoice" without hesitation. In it the tragic realities of human life, such as infant mortality, economic uncertainty, and religious frustration, will not exist.

Chapter 66 returns to the violent, disruptive conditions of the fifth century B.C. (and of human existence generally) to show how God achieves victories even in that milieu, though the rebellion leaves a bitter taste in his mouth (66:24).

The kinds of visionary passages. The overview of ideal or visionary elements in Isaiah has demonstrated their pervasive presence in the book. It has also shown how various are the kinds of visions prevalent there. Some of these varieties may be classified.

The most prevalent is the vision of Yahweh God of Hosts at work in the real world of international politics to bring judgment and salvation. Through the use of this power God deals with Israel and Judah, begins a new age, and restores Zion and the temple as places to which true seekers can go to find him and to worship him. It portrays God as the one who summons the Assyrian as his rod of judgment and Cyrus, the Persian, as the one to restore Zion.

A second picture portrays God dealing with the deteriorated social situation that came from decades of war (chaps. 24–25). The curse of death was in the land and dominated all else. God exercises his sovereign privilege to decree an end to killings and vengeance and an end to the curse that was brought on by the carnage (25:6–9). Sometimes things reach a state of hopelessness where only God's direct sovereign intervention can change them. The Vision believes him capable of such decree.

Another visionary element portrays the Davidic king in the way God wanted him to function (chaps. 9 and 11). It was a vision that could have become a continuing reality in Hezekiah, but the vision only contrasted with Hezekiah's failures to fulfill that role, and the vision of Davidic kingship does not recur in the book.

Another visionary feature is of a totally different society in which there is no violence of any kind (11:6–9 and 65:17–25). This ideal goes beyond even the vision of peace related to the new worship of 2:4 in which disarmament and political peace between nations will be achieved (see also Mic 4:4–5). It recaptures the pastoral scene in Eden again (Genesis 2) where humans and animals are totally at peace with each other.

Another recurrent ideal is one of a nature without desert or destructive elements (34:14–15), which recurs in relation to Israel's return to a devastated Judah (40:4–5; 41:18–19; 42:15–16; 44:23; 55:12–13, and so on.).

A constitutive visionary element is that which pictures the achievement of an open, voluntary, and universal worship of Yahweh in Zion (2:2–4 and chap. 66).

The function of these passages. What function do these passages fill in the Book of Isaiah and in the larger Scriptures? Especially, what do the idealistic passages portraying a completely nonviolent society and a nondestructive nature contribute to the meaning of the book and of Scripture?

The Book of Isaiah and the Bible as a whole show God at work for the redemption of a people, elect and believing. The passages that we have described in Isaiah teach us never to presume that God is "satisfied" with the achievement of certain goals, such as the building of a new temple in Jerusalem or the worship there of a religious remnant of his chosen ones.

God's will moves far beyond that. He holds to the "ideal" and will not settle for a partial, "realistic" achievement. He looks to the redemption of society so that there will be no more violence there. He is determined to achieve the redemption of nature so there will be no more erosion or desert there. He proposes nothing short of a whole new world based on the original model (Genesis 1–2).

God's vision of the world, of society, and of nature has only begun to be fulfilled when a ransomed people are free to worship in Zion's temple (Isaiah 66). Much remains to be achieved before his ideal of a society without violence and a nature without devastation is achieved. Yet the Book of Isaiah proclaims that God who created the heavens and the earth to begin with and who manipulated the empires of history to do his will has the wisdom and the power to accomplish whatever he sets his mind to do.

The New Testament picks up the themes of these passages. It sees beyond Christ's function in personal redemption and redemption of his church and the need for a cosmic redemption. Personal redemption in the midst of a fallen world is glorious, but it is not the whole picture of God's goal. The victory of the "righteous" over the "wicked" is praiseworthy, but it is not complete. The creation of churches as islands of faith in an ocean of social unrest that makes up the world is not enough for God's purposes.

Not until the entire cosmos is redeemed can he be satisfied. That calls for a new heaven and a new earth, with a new nature in which human and animal life are reconciled and complementary, with a new society of tolerance, faith, and peace. Only then can the full heavenly chorus sing the praises of redemption fully achieved. The ideal passages in Isaiah (as in the New Testament) are a reminder of the nature and will of God that cannot be satisfied with anything less.

God's invitations

The Vision documents God's continued welcome to all who would seek him or respond to him. Parallel to admonitions to do God's will are the wonderful invitations. They begin in 1:18-19:

> Come now! Let us test each other,
>   says Yahweh.
> If your sins are like the scarlet robes
>   like the snow they may become white.
> If they are red like crimson,
>   like wool they may become.
> If you become willing and shall obey,
>   the good of the land you may eat!

Provision can be made for forgiveness and atonement, but a willing and obedient spirit is required. God continues to seek such to worship and serve him.

Another invitation was extended to an incredulous Ahaz when Isaiah informed him that his fears were groundless. Only faith is required.

> If you will not believe,
>   certainly you cannot be confirmed! (7:9b)

Yet God offers to encourage that faith:

> Ask for yourself a sign from Yahweh your God, making
>   it deep as Sheol or raising it to a height! (7:11)

Ahaz refuses the offer, but God gives the sign anyway. The required faith is not a test of virtue but a necessity of life with God, and God offers to help it along in any useful way. God only requires a willing and obedient response that only the person can express. The invitations rise from God's will to be gracious to his people and to all who seek him:

> Surely, Yahweh waits to be gracious to you.
> Surely, he rises up to show you mercy,
>   for Yahweh is a God of justice.
> Blessed are all who wait for him! (30:18)

Knowing God

The strongest call for Israel to believe and obey comes in chapters 40–48. The tone is stronger than an invitation. God argues his case with pleas, proofs, and exhortations that Israel is still his servant, even in Babylon, that his salvation is still theirs. In the course of this argument he turns to the peoples of other nations (probably Canaan) with the invitation:

> Turn to me and be saved, all you borderlands!
> For I am God. There is no other. . . .
> For every knee bows to me!
> Every tongue swears (by me)! (45:22–23)

That the invitation is open for any and all who will to share in Israel's blessed estate is even clearer in chapter 55:

> This is the heritage of Yahweh's servants,
>   their right (given) by me.
>   Oracle of Yahweh.
> Hail! Every one who thirsts, come to water!
> And whoever has no money come, buy,
>   without money and without price,
>   wine and milk. . . .
> Turn your ears and come to me.
> Hear that your soul may live.
> And I will make for you an age-long covenant
>   The devotions of David—which are sure. . . .
> Seek Yahweh while he may be found!
>   Call him while he is near!
> May the guilty forsake his way
>   and the troublemaker his convictions.
> And may he turn to Yahweh that he may have
>   compassion on him
>   and to our God that he may multiply pardon.
>   (54:17e–55:1, 3, 6–7)

The invitation is given to everyone. It does not require an ability to pay. It does not exclude guilty sinners or poor suppliants. It does require, as in 1:18, willingness and obedience, and it does call for listening to God's word. The extent of the invitation is made explicit: it includes foreigners and eunuchs:

> Let the foreigner not say
> who has joined himself to Yahweh:
> "Yahweh will certainly keep me separate
> from his people."
> Let the eunuch not say
> "See! I am a dried up tree."
> For thus says Yahweh:
> To the eunuchs who keep my sabbaths
> and who choose what I will
> and who hold fast my covenant:
> I shall give them
> in my house and within my walls
> hand and name.
> Better than sons and daughters,
> an age-long name I give to them
> which will not be cut off. (56:3-5)

This pronouncement makes no judgment on the rights or wrongs of their condition, but it announces God's invitation to participate in his blessings, to minister and worship in Yahweh's name, and to be his servants. They, too, are invited to keep the sabbath and hold fast the covenant.

> Foreigners who are joining themselves to Yahweh
> to minister to him and worship the name of
> Yahweh
> to be his servants,
> everyone keeping sabbath—not profaning it—
> and holding fast my covenant,
> I (will) bring them to my holy mountain
> and make them to rejoice in my house of prayer.
> Their burnt offerings and their sacrifices (are)
> acceptable on my altar.

For my house
is to be called a house of prayer
for all peoples. (56:6-7; WBC 25:250-51)

The basis for the invitation is defined in 57:15 (WBC 25:264):

For thus says the one high and lifted up,
Dweller Forever whose name is Holy:
I dwell in the high and holy place
with one contrite and lowly of spirit
to revive the spirit of (the) humble ones
and to revive the heart of those practicing contrition.

God recognizes the difference between one who errs from his ways for a time, but is redeemable (57:16-19), and those properly called "adversaries" (KJV "the wicked"), who are thus considered incorrigible (57:20-21; WBC 25:264).

The goal of the entire Vision focuses on the new temple in a new Jerusalem where those who respond to God's invitation gather, worship, and serve.

I pay attention to this (one):
to a humble and contrite spirit
who trembles at my word. . . .
Hear the word of Yahweh,
you who tremble at his word!
Look at me extending to her (Jerusalem)
(prosperous) peace like a river
and the glory (wealth) of nations
like an overflowing stream (from which) you
may suckle. . . .
Like a person whose mother comforts (him),
so I myself will comfort you
and with Jerusalem you may (now) be comforted.
(66:2b, 5a, 12, 13)

Refusing the invitation brings dire consequences. Those who reject it are identified as adversaries, rebels against God and his cause.

Even as these have fixed their choice on their own ways
    and their soul delights in their abominations,
so I have fixed my choice on their afflictions
    and bring their worst fears to reality for them.
Because, when I called,
    no one answered.
When I spoke,
    no one heard (me).
Thus they did (what was) evil in my sight,
    and they fixed their choice on that in which I
        took no delight. (66:3e–4; WBC 25:358)

And it will be
    from a new moon to its (following) new moon,
        and from a sabbath to its (following) sabbath,
all flesh will come
    to worship before me,
        says Yahweh.
When they go out, they will look
    at the corpses of persons
        who were rebelling against me.
For their worm will not die
    and their fire will not go out.
        But they will continue to be an abhorrence to all flesh.
                            (66:23–24; WBC 25:366)

KNOWING GOD IN 2
THE WORLD

God is understood in Isaiah to be the sovereign ruler over all his creation and over Canaan particularly. This rule had been assigned to David and his successors on Zion's throne (Psalm 2). The Vision of Isaiah recognizes this assignment, especially in chapters 9 and 11 where the Davidic king was called and established to exercise God's sovereignty over Canaan, its lands, and its kings.

Yet the Vision also recognizes the failure of the monarchy. Northern Israel no longer in any sense represented God's rule in the eighth century and was targeted for destruction (1:4-7; 9:8-10:19). The southern kings also proved unable to follow God's plans; that is, Hezekiah (chap. 22) and Josiah (chaps. 28-33). The role of being ruler on God's behalf passed to the Assyrian. He was to destroy rebellious kingdoms (7:17-10:25). His assignment was specific, negative, and limited in time, but he was clearly God's instrument in a sense formerly reserved for a Davidic king. God is known in this relation to world powers by three names or titles: Yahweh of Hosts, Owner of the Land, and Creator of Heaven and Earth.

One aspect of God's being relates to his being lord and master, sovereign over societies, over nations, and over history. The title "Lord of Hosts," that is, "Lord of Armies," expresses this. Isaiah uses the title throughout. Yahweh is master of Israel, Judah, and Jerusalem, of their peoples, and of their rulers. He establishes their leadership, determines their fate, prospers them with plenty, and judges them with deprivation.

Isaiah understands that this Lordship extends as well to all the small nations in Canaan. That is the basis for the oracles over them in the book: the Philistines (14:29–32), Moab (15:1–16:14), Aram (17:1–8 as also 7:7–9), Phoenicia (23:1–18), and Edom (34:5–15).

Yahweh is also Lord over the great nations beyond. Assyria's rise to power is attributed to Yahweh's decision (8:4–10, 17–24), and his control continues over her (10:5–19; 14:24–27; et passim). Babylon and its king come under Yahweh's judgment (13:1–14:32, 21:1–10). Arabia also earns his wrath (21:11–17), and Egypt and Cush are his concern (chaps. 18–19; et passim).

God uses the nations to accomplish his sovereign will. This is true in his use of Assyria to end the long regimes in Canaanite nations as well as in Israel's Samaria. The Vision of what in God's mind could come to pass (chap. 19) pictures a world in which Egypt, Assyria, and Israel live in prosperous peace, but the most specific example of God's use of a nation is portrayed in his dealing with the Persian rulers, Cyrus and his successors.

Cyrus is raised up and established in power to be God's "servant," even "his anointed." His task is very different from that of God's other "servant," Israel. This task corresponds to God's title as Lord of Hosts. Cyrus has had "his right hand strengthened to subdue nations . . . to open doors . . . [to] level city walls . . . [and] to shatter brass doors and cut apart iron bars" (45:1–2). Here is the picture of God as warrior and conqueror in history, preparing the way for the astonishing rise of Cyrus to power over an empire greater than had ever been known to that time—all "for the sake of my servant, Jacob, Israel, my chosen one" (45:4).

Whereas Israel is called to a spiritual and humble ministry before the Holy One, there is another side to God's relation to his creation. He is cognizant of and master of the use of brute power, whether its form be military, political, or social. God is prepared to use that power fully; he had done so earlier through David (2 Samuel and passim in the Psalms). In Isaiah he is shown to be using that power in the post-Exilic period through the empires, first the Assyrian and then the Persian, to create the conditions in Canaan and Jerusalem that suited his purpose. (Daniel will later apply the same oversight and purpose to the Greek Empire, and John's Apocalypse will apply it to the Romans).

God is a realist, and he knows how to establish and use real political and military power to bring stability and a measure of justice to the time and over the area that he needs. He does so in order to make his holy purposes possible, that his humble servants may exist and do his will.

Cyrus was called and empowered, says the Isaiah passage, "for the sake of my servant Jacob, Israel, my chosen" (45:4). God says:

> I myself have aroused him within my rights
> and I make all his paths straight.
> He builds my city
> and sends out my exiles. (45:13; cf. 44:28)

This is in the context of the reminder:

> I myself have made the earth
> and I have created humankind upon it.
> I stretched out the heavens (with) my own hands
> and I commanded all their legions (of stars). (45:12)

This boggles the mind. The Creator and Lord of history has done all this, creating the world and ordering history, in order for his people to be able to serve and worship him properly!

God's actions in directing history use the term "right," "righteous," or "within my rights" (55:13). Also the word "salvation" appears regularly with it (45:8bc). The expressions assert God's "right" to regulate the nations as over against any perception of the "rights" of national deities and of the "right" he gives them to exercise authority over other nations. This particularly applies to their right to exercise dominion in Canaan, Yahweh's particular territory, and over peoples that Yahweh through David had claimed as his own. God gives Cyrus, then Darius, and then Artaxerxes legitimacy as his own agents to maintain civil order and to rebuild his temple city, Jerusalem (cf. WBC 25:133-35, 158-62).

The one or other nation that is to carry out the Lord of Host's will in ruling and building, in maintaining civil order and freedom of worship, is chosen for the task and granted God's own legitimacy. That nation or its ruler is God's tool for this purpose. To assume that the nation or ruler is more than this is to invite rejection and humiliation (8:5-19; 13:17-19). These rulers and nations are tools in the hands of God to fulfill his plan, to accomplish his purpose (14:24-27). They are considered "legitimate" or "righteous" only so long as they are accomplishing that purpose, which is to achieve "salvation" for God's own people.

There are clearly two aspects of God's relation to people in this world. The central one is expressed by Isaiah in the title "The Holy One of Israel." The second is found in the title "The Lord of Hosts." Yahweh covers both.

The Lord of Hosts corresponds to God's sovereignty over history and all the forces that compete in that arena: over kings and nations, armies and empires, governments and societies. God uses these to create the conditions within which the humble may worship and serve. He also changes leadership and power to suit his purpose. Isaiah shows God's work stretching over centuries of time; the view from any one person's lifetime is bound to be partial and distorted.

The owner of "the land"

Eras change some of the basic axioms within which faith operates. A basic assumption in the Pentateuch, particularly Deuteronomy, and in Israel's orientation generally before the Exile, was that the Lord intended all of Canaan to belong to Israel. The Law was given at Sinai but intended to regulate life "in the land" (see "Excursus: The Land" WBC 24:316–27).

The Lord's promise to Abraham included the people and "the land." Deuteronomy and Joshua see "the land" as clearly distinct from Israel. It was already Yahweh's land before Israel arrived. It was "a land the Lord your God cares for. The eyes of the Lord your God are continually on it from the beginning of the year to its end. I send rain on your land" (Deut 11:10–12). It was a land inhabited by peoples of seven different ethnic groups (Deut 6:10, 23; 7:1) whom the Lord promised to drive out (Deut 11:23). The extent of "the land" is defined: "from the desert to Lebanon and from the Euphrates to the western sea" (Deut 11:24, NIV). Deuteronomy recognizes that Israel's life "in the land" is contingent on maintaining covenant (Deut 4:26). It also recognizes that Israel in Exile far from the land may still seek the Lord and find him (Deut 4:29).

It is against this background that the Vision of Isaiah begins to deal with the Exilic situation in which a large proportion of Israel is no longer in the land and in which Persian control is complete and apparently permanent. It moves to counter the hope expressed in Deuteronomy and Jeremiah that Israel's future lay in a return to "the land" and a restoration of the monarchy.

Isaiah does not continue the assumption that Israel's future and the future of "the land" are inextricably linked or that the Torah can only be observed "in the land." It shows how Yahweh's judgment has fallen on "the land" through the Assyrian armies. Repeated incursions devastated the nations that lived there: the Philistine cities (14:28-32); Moab (chaps. 15-16); the Arameans of Damascus (chap. 7); Edom (21:11-12); and Tyre (chap. 23). The total devastation of "the land" is mourned in chapter 24 (see WBC 24:313-22).

Yahweh's judgment fell on "the land" and "the peoples of the land," more precisely called "the border lands" (or "the ends of the earth") and "the coastal lands" (or "the islands of the sea"). This judgment is a part of God's action to end Davidic claims to be their liege-lord. The nations now become vassals of Assyria, Babylon, and Persia, as do Israel and Judah.

When God's new era for Israel and Jerusalem is hailed (chaps. 40-48), these borderlands and coastal lands are called to be witnesses (41:1, 5) and to be saved (45:22). The lands are invited to send representatives to worship in Jerusalem's new temple (66:18) as more distant peoples (66:19) are also called.

This represents a fundamental difference from Deuteronomy's attitude toward these peoples. Instead of eliminating or driving them from the land, they are to be welcomed at Jerusalem's festivals. Ezra still represents the exclusiveness of Deuteronomy (cf. Ezra 9), but Isaiah represents a very different accepting attitude.

Note that the direction of movement in Isaiah 66 is toward Jerusalem. The New Testament will recognize a new era and a counterflow away from Jerusalem to Judea-Samaria and to the "ends of the land" (or "the earth") (Acts 1:8). Jesus spoke to the Samaritan woman of a day to come when "neither at this mountain nor in Jerusalem" would worship be done, but "in spirit and in truth" (John 4:21). Isaiah's trend is a step away from the identity of Israel's hope with "the land" to a recognition of a legitimate place for Judaism out in the world, even while a rebuilt Jerusalem remains its symbolic center. The New Testament takes one step further in which even that geographic center is removed. The center of future attention will be the heavenly Jerusalem (Rev 21:1-4), which parallels in wording many pictures in Isaiah.

Isaiah seems to be saying that the Torah's linkage of Israel's life to "the land" belonged to the former age. God may well be "the owner of the land," but his plans for Israel now involve his larger dominion. His use of the Persian emperors to rebuild the city of Jerusalem and bring order in "the land" still show his concern, but Israel now functions on a different level.

The Creator of the heavens and the earth

Every student of Hebrew is aware that the word "create" in Genesis 1 is a rare word used only with God as subject. The highest concentration of uses of that word occurs in Isaiah 40-66. If there should be any fear that Isaiah's emphasis on God as the owner of Canaan represents a provincial and limited picture of God, this fact should dispel it.

The Vision begins with a disputation in which God accuses his people. For this he summons the Heavens and the Earth as witnesses (1:2; WBC 25:93-94). When he is trying to persuade Israel in Exile that he is arranging historical forces to help them achieve his destined goals for them, he reminds them that he created the universe (40:26, 28; 42:5; 45:7, 18). In powerful poetic images he pictures his own great being and power by contrasting it with the stars of the heaven that are as particles of dust. The figure has only gained in meaning for our generation with our telescopes and moon walks. We sing "How Great Thou Art!" and "He's Got the Whole World in His Hands" in response to just this teaching.

The point of these references in Isaiah is to insist that the One who created the universe is great enough and skilled enough to manipulate historical forces to benefit his people if he so desires. God uses this creative power to provide the means for Israel's return and to encourage Jerusalem (41:20;

48:7). These two passages frame the long section (chaps. 40–48) in which God appeals to Israel in exile to recognize their privileged position as his servants and to cooperate with his plan to redeem them. He pictures this effort to save them as a kind of new Exodus, recalling the miraculous and improbable event that was established in Jewish minds as the ultimate picture of salvation (Exod 6:1–15:21). God does not depend on favorable circumstances. He creates the events he needs to accomplish his purposes. One may call them miracles. They testify to the sovereign, creative power of God to save.

Israel's very existence is witness to God's creation of her through all he has done (43:1, 7, 15). She, like the universe and mankind, is a product of God's creation. She reflects God's intentional, formative, constituting action, just as the creation of the world does.

The heart of this section (chaps. 40–48) is chapter 45 which proclaims God's choice of Cyrus to redeem Israel and restore Jerusalem. This chapter makes the awesome claim that Yahweh, Israel's God, set the events in motion that brought the Persian prince to be king of the Medes and the Persians and then to the conquest of all the territories from India's border on the east to Greece on the west and Egypt in the southwest, with the specific purpose of having him restore Jerusalem and making it possible for Jews to worship there. All world history becomes a frame for God's appearance to meet his worshipers in Jerusalem (chap. 66).

In making his call to Cyrus, God pictures himself as Creator. He insists that he alone is God and that his rule is universal (45:5–6). Then he says:

> Former of light,
>   creator of darkness,
> maker of peace,
>   creator of violence,
> I am Yahweh,
>   maker of all these. (45:7)

The claim is even more universal than that in Genesis 1. There Yahweh is portrayed as creator of all the positive things, such as order and light and dry land. Here God claims to originate both the positive and the negative. He controls both "light" and "darkness," both "peace" and "violence."

Then God pictures his work through Cyrus in parallel terms with his creation of the world.

> I myself have made the earth
> and I have created humankind upon it.
> I stretched out the heavens (with) my own hands
> and I commanded all of their legions (of stars).
> I myself have aroused him (Cyrus) within my rights
> and I make all his ways straight.
> He builds my city
> and he sends out my exiles
> with neither bribe
> nor reward,
> says Yahweh of Hosts. (45:12–13)

The speech identifies God, Lord of history, with God, Redeemer of Israel, and both with God, the Creator of all that exists. This magnificent and comprehensive statement shows how God's extensive power in creation is a macrocosm of his work in history and of his work in the election and redemption of Israel. He creates all of it.

Then the climax of God's creative work in Isaiah comes in "a new heaven and a new land," in a Jerusalem which elicits joy and gladness (65:17–18). God's goals for his creation are also brought to accomplishment by his creative power when all things are created new. Our hope for the present and the future are based on the faith that God, the beneficent creator, is at work now and will bring all things to his desired end. John uses the same faith for his climactic chapter when God says "I am making everything new" (Rev 21:5, NIV). That also includes "heaven and earth" and "Jerusalem."

Our hope rests on the belief that God, our Savior, is also creator of all things. In this chaotic world there is no ultimate hope in the constancy of nature or the goodness of historical processes. Hope is found now as it was for Exilic Israel in Isaiah's firm conviction that God's creative power which shaped the universe is directed toward redemption and a new creation in which we are invited to participate. That is grounds for "joy and gladness" indeed (65:18-19).

KNOWING GOD AMONG   3
HIS OWN PEOPLE

The Holy One of Israel

Gen 1:27 refers to man created in God's image. "Image" refers to a likeness made by casting or shaping by a form or mold. The product is not the same as the form, but is instead the opposite of the form, corresponding and fitting to it. Can it be that "created in God's image" means, not that man is like God, but that man corresponds negatively to God? What God is, man is not? What man is, God is not? Do the opposites correspond to each other?

Whatever may be the case in Genesis, there is no doubt that the prophets stress these differences. God exclaims: "I am God and not man" (Hos 11:9b). Isa 2:10–18 expounds man's tendency to be proud and arrogant when in fact only God can be properly exalted and high. Humanity that does not accept the fact that God is to be exalted and humans are to be humble must experience humiliation; God alone is to be exalted.

This polar contrast is expressed throughout the Vision of Isaiah by the term for God "the Holy One of Israel" and by the recognition that the proper attitude and position for his worshiper is humility with a contrite demeanor.

God's holiness is best experienced and understood in the sanctuary where careful controls limit contact between the holy and anything or anyone profane. Yet the sanctuary makes contact possible in worship between the Holy God and the less holy suppliant. This was true in the Tabernacle of Exodus-Leviticus and in Solomon's temple. Isaiah portrays a time and place when Jerusalem will fulfill these functions (2:2–4 and chaps. 65–66). The book is not as concerned with sacrifice and priestly ordinances as Leviticus, but it is fully aware of the issues relating to God's holiness.

God was outraged by the violation of Jerusalem's holy precincts through violence and injustice (1:10–15, 21–25). The threefold *sanctus*, "Holy, Holy, Holy," greets the prophet at the entrance to God's heavenly court (6:3) and brings immediate recognition of uncleanness which must be purged. And so it is throughout the book. God is holy. This aspect of God's being must be met by contrition and worship.

One responds to this by seeking God in his holy place. This is done through pilgrimages to Jerusalem in 2:2–4 and in 66:19–21. Experiencing God's presence in the Holy City is open to everyone: to Israelites wherever they are as well as those from the nations (Gentiles) who wish to worship him. The journey and the worship exercises are expressions of humility and contrition that are appropriate and appreciated by the Holy One of Israel.

The theme, however, is expressed elsewhere. God's holiness is visualized in his being exalted. His city is exalted above all the mountains (2:2). His throne is "high and exalted" (6:1). He dwells in "a high and holy place" (57:15b). But he does not dwell there alone. He seeks worshipers in these places to share his presence, those who can fit that relation, who are "humble and lowly in spirit" (57:15b).

Those who climb the mountain in 2:2–4 seeking God, his instruction, and his justice are those who want to "walk in his ways" (2:3b). The prophet in God's throne room knows contrition for his condition and seeks relief from it (6:5). Only then is he prepared to be God's messenger with a harsh and difficult message (6:8–13). The "servants of Yahweh" who are invited to God's free feast of all good things are not the good; they are the repentant and contrite (55:7). God recognizes the difference between himself and them (55:8–9) but holds out his open invitation to all, including the eunuch and the foreigner who in humility can maintain justice (56:1) and keep the sabbath (56:2). He wants his temple to be known as "a house of prayer for all nations" (56:7c).

This is the spirit and attitude of the chosen one who sings:

> The Spirit of my Lord Yahweh is on me
>   because Yahweh has anointed me.
> To bring good news to poor persons, he has sent me,
> to bandage one with broken hearts,
> to proclaim liberty to captives
>   and an opening to those imprisoned,
> to proclaim the year of Yahweh's favor
>   and our God's day of vengeance,
> to comfort all mourners. (61:1–2)

These words are positioned in the Vision at a place that may represent Ezra's mission. They were appropriated by our Lord Jesus Christ as descriptive of his own mission (Luke 4:14–21). The humility reflected in these words, like that of the humbled teacher in 50:4–9 and the one slain in the service of Yahweh (53:3–5) and of the prophet (6:5), is characteristic of the humility expected of anyone serving the Holy One of Israel.

But this is also true of every worshiper of the Holy God, not only of the leaders.

> For thus says one high and lifted up,
>   Dweller Forever whose name is Holy:
> I dwell in the high and holy place
>   with one contrite and lowly of spirit

to revive the spirit of humble ones
and to revive the heart of those practicing contrition.
(57:15)

This is in contrast to those pagans who establish "their bed on a mountain, high and lifted up, and who go up there to sacrifice" (56:7). The pagan exalts himself; God's kind of worshiper humbles himself or herself and thus qualifies for an exalted place where the truly Exalted One, the Holy One of Israel, lives.

For the new temple in a new city that God is having made in Jerusalem, he announces:

I pay attention to this (one):
to a humble and contrite spirit
who trembles at my word. (66:2b)

The one who fits the mold, who is indeed in the image of God as his counterpart, matches humility and contrition to God's holy exaltation. In this, creation is perfected and crowned.

God in Zion

There is no more than a hint in the Pentateuch that God has any special interest in Jerusalem. Early in Abram's sojourn in Canaan he meets a certain Melchizedek, king of Salem, and receives his blessing (Gen 14:18-20). That is all.

David's conquest of Jerusalem and his determination to build a temple to Yahweh in his capitol (2 Samuel 6-7) changed that. The temple and the city, as they are celebrated in the Psalms, become a central focus for biblical worship and piety. The temple takes the place and function of the Torah's tabernacle (Exodus 25-40) and the sacrifices authorized there (Leviticus 1-16) as well as for the priesthood instituted there.

Knowing God among His Own People

When the prophetic books refocus Israel's faith for the new era in which they no longer have a land or country of their own, Jerusalem assumes a central role. The restoration of the temple (Haggai and Zechariah 1-8) and the later restoration of the whole city (Ezra-Nehemiah) become the goals of Judaism that give them a central and unifying focus.

In these developments the Bible also comes to emphasize an understanding of God as the one who is present and revealed in Zion and in Zion's worship forms. As such, the experience of seeing and worshiping God in Jerusalem's temple becomes the prototype for all liturgical and worship forms used by those who depend on the Bible for inspiration and direction. Isaiah is a pivotal book in shaping this view of "God who dwells in Zion."

God's attitude toward Jerusalem in the eighth century is described in chapter 1. The ravages of invasion leave Zion isolated and exposed (1:8), and the fact that she continues to exist at all is due to God's grace (1:9). The verses could be a summation of the situation pictured in chapters 36-37 and 2 Kgs 18-19 (WBC 24:38, 124).

To this Jerusalem, God addresses words of correction and of invitation. He rejects their idea that worship for Yahweh consists in blood sacrifice (1:11-15). Instead he calls for purity and justice (1:16-17). He insists that sins can be forgiven (1:18). What is essential is willingness and obedience, desire and discipline. Refusal and rebellion are intolerable (1:19-20). Unfortunately, Jerusalem at that time does not represent these essential elements.

A vision follows of what Zion and worship there must become (2:2-4). It will be elevated so that "all nations," "many peoples," will be drawn to it. It will be known as "the mountain of Yahweh," the place where "the house of the God of Jacob" is. Worship is portrayed as receiving instruction in the ways of God so that worshipers may "walk in his paths." Then Zion is identified as the place from which Torah (instruction or possibly the Pentateuch) comes, the place where "the word of Yahweh" may be heard. There nations and peoples may be affirmed by God in ways of peace.

This description stands in contrast to the Jerusalem of 1:10–23. It also stands in contrast to David's Jerusalem, which was the capital from which his conquering armies moved, or Solomon's Jerusalem, which was the headquarters for a small empire taxing and controlling almost all of Canaan ("the land"). To change the Jerusalem of 1:10–23 into that of 2:2–4 would take patience and would be a long process. The Vision of Isaiah recounts the process: 3:1–4:1 describes the disintegration of the old systems, 4:2–6 describes in symbolic terms the caustic cleansing of the city and the creation of a protective canopy for the holy city.

The Zion that the Psalms present is one in which God's authority over the nations (that is, over history) is experienced as the Davidic ruler is authenticated in his role and function. He is also experienced in many other legitimate ways as well. Isaiah's vision of Zion is a real possibility for post-Exilic Israel, where the older idea is no longer a possibility for them. The Vision suggests that God himself is responsible for the change. He is not a victim of circumstance and historical change, but the creator, the initiator of the events that make the difference. The resulting possibility of worship in Zion is what he wants.

To arrive at this he eliminates the nationalistic and political element from that worship. The royal persons and offices that existed in eighth-century Jerusalem (chaps. 7–9) are no longer a part of the picture after chapter 40. These powers and responsibilities are transferred to the emperor (chap. 45). He must make worship in Jerusalem possible by maintaining order, building roads, and providing material resources as well as granting permission for the building of the temple and the city. Yet there is to be no hint of emperor worship there ("neither bribe nor reward" [45:13; WBC 25:288]).

To experience the presence of God in Zion meant being ready to be taught, being open to instruction in the ways of

God, being prepared to live out those instructions ("to walk in his ways") and to live in an intense and intimate sense of his presence as a "humble and contrite" devotee who is content to share his presence and experience his holy glory. To experience the powerful presence of God in Zion meant to recognize that worshipers on the right and on the left—even some who led the worship—come from different nations and peoples. The God of Zion is God of the whole earth, the only true God for all peoples.

As worship on Zion is separated from the political and social processes, Isaiah portrays it as more intensely related to the mystery of creation and to the ultimate values of "light and darkness," "good and evil." God in Zion controlled and determined these things.

Holy Spirit

God, or his applied leading and power, is referred to repeatedly as "spirit" in Isaiah. The term is descriptive of the way in which God is experienced and understood as he is at work in the world and in history.

In 4:4 God's judgment on Jerusalem is called "a spirit of judgment and a spirit of burning." The description is of the cleansing and purging word of God. Because of this work of God's spirit, the people of God's city of the future can be called "holy." In this way the judgments of God are portrayed with a positive goal and function (WBC 24:50).

Similarly, the use of human leaders by God is performed through the work and presence of God's spirit. This is shown fully in the beautiful picture of the promised Davidic king (11:2):

> The spirit of Yahweh shall rest on him:
>   a spirit of wisdom and understanding,
> a spirit of counsel and heroism,
>   a spirit of knowledge, and fear, of Yahweh.

The gifts that a successful king needs, which make rule and genuine commitment to God possible, are not character attributes inherent in the person. They are products of God's gift of his spirit. Pss 51:12[10], 13[11], 14[12], 19[17] parallel Isaiah's emphasis. There is an echo of the view of kingship that was present in 1 Sam 10:6, 10; 11:6; 16:13, 14; 19:9. Being of the elect line of David was not enough; one needed to be empowered and directed by God's spirit (WBC 24:171-72).

The spirit of God directs the Persian emperors, Cyrus (42:1-4; WBC 24:119) and Artaxerxes (59:19; WBC 24:287). This statement as much as any other marks the change in God's plan. What was the understanding of a special relation to a Davidic ruler before becomes the unction granted the emperors to carry out God's wishes. They owe their success and skill to God.

The spirit is claimed by post-Exilic leaders. In 48:16, Sheshbazzar says, "The Lord Yahweh has sent me—and his spirit" (WBC 25:178). In 61:1, another (possibly Ezra) says, "The spirit of my Lord Yahweh is on me, because Yahweh has anointed me." The speech goes on to spell out his tasks (WBC 25:302).

The New Testament shows a similar relation between Jesus and God's spirit. Jesus claims the passage from Isa 61:1-3 to be descriptive of his own mission (Luke 4:12-21). Luke portrays his ministry as "full of the Holy Spirit (Luke 4:1). Mark describes Jesus' baptism in terms of "the spirit descending on him like a dove" (Mark 1:10).

Isaiah portrays God's spirit active in the redemption of the whole people, "until spirit is poured upon us from above" (32:15-20). The enabling spirit of God will equip and empower the entire people as was promised for the Davidic king (WBC 24:417). God promises, "I pour my spirit on your seed" (44:3). His spirit brings revival and new life in place of "a spirit of fainting" (61:3).

The spirit of God is also understood to have prepared the scroll of judgment for Edom and the nations (34:16). Its work is parallel to Yahweh's express command. In 40:7, the understanding of spirit in relation to judgment (4:4) is used in a skeptical question about the weakness of humanity in God's presence:

> Grass withers,
> a flower fades
> when the spirit of Yahweh
> blows against it. (40:7)

But the answer relates "spirit" to "the word of God" to emphasize its trustworthiness. "Spirit" is not just wind and power; it includes the will and understanding of God. It is controlled by the plan and purpose of God (WBC 25:82).

The very next passage equates the inscrutability and incomprehensibility of Yahweh's spirit as, indeed, of his own being:

> Who can gauge Yahweh's spirit?
> Or instruct him as his personal counselor?
> (40:13; WBC 25:90–91)

The Spirit of God here includes his mind, purpose, and plans, as well as his motivation and intended implementation.

PART 2
SERVING GOD AND HIS PLAN

4   INTRODUCTION

In the Israelite monarchy the servant of Yahweh was understood to be the king. David and his successors combined within their person and function all the counterparts to the revealed God of Israel that were discussed in the first part of this book. The Davidic king was God's representative in ruling Canaan and all its peoples and nations. The full and real exercise of this power had slipped very badly between Solomon and Uzziah, but the symbol was still there.

The Davidic king was patron of Jerusalem and of its temple. He was responsible for the safety and worship of the city. In the monarchy, the Davidic king was the person responsible for the covenant Israel had with God, as Josiah's hearing of the read Torah implies. He was also the model of the individual worshiper, as the large number of "laments of the individual" in the Psalter shows.

With the division of the kingdom under Rehoboam, some of this began to unravel. By the end of the reign of Uzziah (late eighth century B.C.), the rising power of Assyria was beginning to be felt in Canaan. One way to view the message of the Book of Isaiah would be to study the way the roles of the servant of Yahweh, once inherent in the Davidic king, are redistributed in the period from the eighth century to after the Exile. The governing functions of servanthood had to make place for the Assyrian before the Exile and for the Persian afterward. The place of the Davidic king and his descendants is thus made subordinate with much narrower functions.

Worship in Jerusalem is corrupt at the beginning. Israel has lost its reason for being, and the individual worshiper is adrift and vulnerable. The worshiping functions of servanthood are redistributed to Israel in Exile, to a restored Jerusalem, and those who in humility see God's presence.

The latter part of Isaiah's vision makes explicit what is implicit throughout: God has a purpose or strategy in mind for history and the world. Likewise, persons and societies are judged by their usefulness to that strategy. For that they should be "willing and obedient" (1:19), but too often they "resist and rebel" (1:20).

The kingdoms of Israel and Judah do not conform to God's strategy and have to be eliminated along with many of their neighbors. In fact an entire civilization (42:9; 43:18–19) is brought to an end and replaced for this reason.

So the latter part of the book sets out to define who is a servant of Yahweh, what his purpose is, and what such a one should do. At least five forms of servanthood emerge. Some of them are surprising. The older strategy had been to fulfill the promise to Abraham by having God's people in God's land fulfill God's purpose through covenant. This took form first in the tribal league (Joshua–Judges) and then of a single kingdom with Jerusalem as its capitol (1 Samuel–1 Kings 9). This form splintered and finally collapsed.

The new strategy is revealed in Isaiah. It centers in establishing Jerusalem as a temple city to which scattered Israel as well as those who wish from all those countries might come to worship (2:2–4; 40:9–11; 65:17–66:24). God uses a variety of servants to accomplish this. At the same time, they need to be in agreement with this strategy and obedient to God's terms for achieving it. Those called include the descendants of ancient Israel, the rulers of the Persian and presumably succeeding empires, the people of Jerusalem, submissive, suffering individuals, and the humble, contrite people from all nations who come to Jerusalem to worship and to learn.

With all of this God faces a problem. There are those who are identified as persistent rebels against God's ways and plans. Old Israel is one who is unknowing and cannot understand (1:2–7; 2:6–8). The old Jerusalem is compared with Sodom and Gomorrah (1:10) whose worship is totally unacceptable (1:11–25). All the proud and arrogant of mankind come under similar judgment (2:10–22).

In the "former times" the king of Babylon (13:1–14:32; 21:1–10) and Hezekiah (chap. 22) are singled out as persistent rebels. In the latter times Exilic Israel seems to resist God's call (chaps. 40–48), while Jerusalem's inhabitants join in persecuting the suffering servant (chaps. 50 and 53) and are reluctant to accept God's challenge in chapter 54. Others are recalcitrant in chapters 57, 59, and 65, while some actively resist the restoration in 66:3b–6. The bitterness of this continued resistance is reflected in the book's last verse (66:24). God's strategy and his call to participate in its accomplishment divides the people and the nations. God's pleas are not successful in persuading them to unite in serving him.

A matter of divine decision

The Book of Isaiah assumes throughout that God controls the destinies of persons, families, and nations. It sees this control used, not capriciously, but always to work out his strategy, to achieve his goals. The book uses the word *pāqad*, meaning "to determine the fate of," to describe this; it has often been translated "visit" or "punish" (see WBC 24:325–26). It defines God's decision as to what will happen to a person or a group in a given situation or time, whether they will be blessed or cursed, pushed into battle or rescued from danger, granted rain and prosperity or condemned to drought and deprivation. God is a sovereign making decisions and putting them into effect.

In chapter 10 Israel's fate is determined: destruction by the Assyrians. Chapter 6 had already spelled out the extent of that decision. Chapter 1 spoke of the effects of this destiny on Israel and of the different decision about Jerusalem (see also chap. 4). The fate of the entire land of Canaan is fixed because of evil and sin (13:11), as is that of different ethnic groups and nations (chaps. 13-21). The height of negative decisions falls in chapters 23-27: Tyre's destiny is fixed for seventy years (23:17); the armies of the highlands and the kings of the lowlands will have their fates similarly decided (24:22). In chapter 26 Yahweh has determined the fate of tyrants (v 14) and determined Israel's destiny even in the time of her distress (v 16). He will determine the fate of the people of the land of Canaan in accordance with their sins (v 21). He will also determine the fate of Leviathan (21:1), whatever that name refers to (see WBC 24:348). The emphasis throughout is on God's sovereignty. He is in full charge of things even as everything seems to be falling apart. He is the Lord of life and death (chap. 26; see "Excursus: Yahweh and Death," WBC 24:343), over curse and blessing (WBC 24:317), over the land and mankind. The fate of all fits together in God's work to achieve his strategy.

To bring about an entirely new era God must rearrange older accounts and relationships and establish new ones. His former relationship of patronage to "the land" of Canaan is effectively closed out, as chapter 24 demonstrates. The same is true of his relation to the kingdom of northern Israel (Samaria) and of Judah as a kingdom. His relation to Israel and Jerusalem, however, simply takes on new forms, as we shall see. God adopts the Assyrians to demolish the established political systems of Canaan and the Persians to build new ones. He decrees humiliation to the proud and exalted of mankind (chap. 2) and elevation for the humble and the contrite (chap. 57). God, and God alone, determines fate, and he does so with an eye on his goals and strategies, as well as on permanent principles and values.

With the whole of history in God's sovereign control, with his strategies of creation, election, and grace, one might wonder why all the world is not the garden of Eden (Genesis 2) or the realm of peace and order that so perfectly reflects his purpose (Isa 11:6-9; 34:1-10; 65:20-25). The Book of Isaiah, like Genesis 3 and 4, points to God's problem: his human creation, called and blessed, won't cooperate. They refuse and rebel (1:20); they "do not know or understand" (1:3); they are proud and arrogant (2:11-17a, 22; WBC 24:17).

God's problem exists with the peoples in the land of Canaan (Philistines, Edom, Moab, Aram, Sidon, and Tyre), with distant kings and nations (Babylon and Egypt), with Israel and Judah, and with Jerusalem and her kings. Nevertheless, it continues with Israel in Exile and the remnant left in Jerusalem. There are some who never give up, resisting to the end (66:24). God has no choice but to condemn these to death and destruction if he is to get on with his beneficent and healing strategies for his people and for all peoples.

Theology may think of God's grace for all his creatures regardless of their response if God is perceived as having no purpose or strategy for society or history. Yet when God's creative and sovereign work is seen to be purposeful and directed, when human destiny is seen as linked to that purpose and persons are called to cooperative work in relation to God's creation, his society, his history, then one must make room for God's response to opposition, refusal, rebellion, and usurpation of his functions. The Book of Isaiah is aware of these conditions within Israel and without and assumes that God will ultimately have to deal with them in order to achieve his goals and to claim his own who are "willing and obedient" (1:18a), "humble and meek" (66:2b), "contrite and lowly" (57:15b), and who "make God their refuge" (56:13c).

God's problem exists with the people of the Northern Kingdom who not only fail to recognize their destiny (1:2) but actively oppose Jerusalem (7:1-9). They had long since divided the nation when Jeroboam rebelled against Rehoboam. They are doomed and must be destroyed (1:2-7; 9:1-10:34).

Rebellion was also present in a Jerusalem that became corrupt and disorderly, in its priests and inhabitants, and had to be purged and renewed (1:8-31; 3:1-4:6; 54:1-17; 61:1-62:12). Many things had to change before the new city could be ready for true worship (2:1-4). Even as it is being prepared to receive the pilgrims, elements of paganism (65:3-5, 11-12) and resistance (66:3-4, 5b-6) are active in the city and its vicinity. Remains of the Lord's judgment are observed by all who come to worship (66:24).

This sad and depressing realism pervades the book. In the midst of the hopeful and encouraging vision of God's determined purpose of grace for Jerusalem, his people, and indeed all nations, there is the persistent reminder that not everyone is willing to participate, not even all of Israel or Jerusalem (65:13-16). For a great part of the book "Israel" and "Jerusalem" are seen as collective terms of elect groups that God wills to save. In the end, however, it becomes clear that incorrigible, self-willed, and determined opponents to God's strategy remain. They will not be there for the festival of faith. They cannot be a part of God's party.

Only by moving to eliminate elements of the opposition (the nation of Israel, other nations in Palestine, Babylon, etc., and individuals of the new age who cannot adapt) can God move on to establish his city as a refuge for the meek and contrite who want to share his presence and to cooperate in his plan. The establishment of a new age, the reformation of political structures and powers, and the reconstitution of Jerusalem were not enough. The called and chosen people who had received so much from God were still divided. There were persistent elements of "dross" or impurities in the fine metal. They still made trouble and had to be separated out (65:13-16). Such were still there in New Testament churches (see 1-2 Corinthians and Revelation 1-3) and presumably are still there today.

Time is of great concern to all of us. For God it is an
instrument to be used to serve his purpose. It is treated seri-
ously in the Book of Isaiah. Blocks of time are called "ages"
('ôlām). God's strategies are designed for such ages or epochs.
The Book of Isaiah implies a kind of unity of consistency for
God's strategy during a period from the sons of Noah to the
present and likens the turmoil of the sixth century B.C. to that
of Noah and the flood (54:9). God promises that the consistency with which he held to his promises after the flood
will be matched by his constancy in relations and forms beginning in this new age of new covenants (54:10). So the new
age, characterized by secular imperial government and by
Jerusalem's role in drawing pilgrim worshipers form all nations and peoples is seen as different from the former times
(WBC 25:120, 237).

To understand God's plan and strategy the Book of Isaiah
teaches that one must look to the long periods of time. His
strategy belongs to the ages; there is development and movement. The book depicts twelve generations over some three
centuries. To make sense of history one must think in terms
of centuries and ages; only then can God's plan and strategy
be understood.

It is futile to try to live, believe, and behave in terms that fit
another time. The period covered by the Vision of Isaiah
(eighth to fifth centuries B.C.) is different from the times of
Abraham, or of Joshua, or of David. For Israel to try to act as
though she were still in those periods ignores the changes
that God has instituted and the new strategies that he is im-
plementing. When Hezekiah or Josiah try to act like David or
Joshua, they are rebuked and defeated. This is a different
time, and there are different factors at work, all of which God
has ordained and determined.

Early Christianity lived under conditions not unlike those
of post-Exilic Israel. They lived under an empire. They devel-
oped congregations. They used the Scriptures. One basic

factor, important to Isaiah, is eliminated in their time: Jerusalem is destroyed and not replaced. This affected both Jews and Christians and changed the direction to which Isaiah had pointed.

Living between the times

Ecclesiastes meditates on the problems of time (8:6-8 et passim). Walt Whitman understood that nineteenth-century America was a time "between things ended and things begun" ("A Clear Midnight"). A great deal of the Book of Isaiah depicts the generations that lived and worked "between the times," that is, between the time God made his decision to change the ages and strategies and the time when the new age was in full effect. Those three centuries "between the times" were full of ambiguity as persons tried to find their way, when so many things had changed and the old landmarks were apparently no longer valid. Some unexpected ones succeeded. Some, surprisingly, failed. All were called to heed the "signs of the times." None was given the key to the future.

Many readers of the Book of Isaiah will feel that the passages that relate to "living between the times" are relevant to this present age. Christians feel the tension of looking back to the life, death, and resurrection of Jesus and forward to his return: living between the times. Israel's wilderness travel between Sinai and Canaan (Numbers 10–Joshua 6) is a paradigm of the period in Isaiah between Uzziah's time (chap. 6) and the coming of Cyrus (chap. 45).

Chapter 6 shows that God's blessing of power and leadership has been taken away from Israel and Jerusalem and given to others. Chapter 10 identifies the Assyrians as the recipient of God's support. Judah's problem and that of her kings becomes that of learning how to live with this strange matter "between the times." The Book of Isaiah suggests that the ones who did so successfully were not the ones who history and the religious society may have viewed as successful. Living under the curse between the times requires some skills that the driving energies of "successful" leaders do not include. So the strong, the proud, the arrogant, the patriotic, and the visionary of days of glory do not do well. The meek, the accepting, the humble, the acquiescing, quiet persons often do much better.

So it is that Hezekiah (chaps. 22 and 36–39) and Josiah (chaps. 28–33), who are elsewhere portrayed as national heroes (2 Kings 18–20 and 22–23, respectively), are kings who are humiliated and unsuccessful in Isaiah. On the other hand, Ahaz (chaps. 7–14) and Manasseh (by implication in chaps. 23–27), who are vilified in 2 Kings 16 and 21, are successful in keeping their thrones in extremely difficult periods. They are humiliated and accept very humble positions for themselves and their country, but they act in accordance with their times, that is, they relate as best they can to God's decreed change in their status and mission.

In a similar way a martyred leader is exalted in chapters 50 and 53 and a lone voice is honored in chapter 61 in contrast with the strident rebels that speak so forcefully in chapters 57–58 and 63–64. Lessons for living "between the times" include taking the risk of faith (7:9b, 10–14; see WBC 24:321, 94), living the promise, and hoping for the King/Messiah (WBC 24:98–102).

While "living between the times, we are challenged to recognize God's sovereign grace even in the most difficult experiences (chaps. 23–24; WBC 24:298–300). God rules over both life and death (25:7–8), and he can protect his people from everything demonic (27:1). The hope for God's grace toward his people will ultimately prove justified (27:12–13).

GOVERNING SERVANTS   5
AND THEIR SERVICE

God's strategy

Knowing that God has a goal and a strategy for achieving that goal through persons, through society, through history, and through worship leads to the recognition that God seeks those who will work with him toward those goals and within the bounds set by that strategy. It also makes clear that there are many who insist on setting other goals which are not from God and on using means other than those prescribed by God.

God needs servants at every level and in every part of life. This includes government and its use of force to maintain order and to build cities and roads. It centers in worship with its cultivation of the sense of God's presence, holiness, and mercy. It assumes God's control of all things, his choice of his servants, his appointment, call, and empowerment of his servants, and his recognition and reward of these servants. The Book of Isaiah develops each of these.

God's work in nature needs servants, too, but the Vision is content to describe God in control of fertility and prosperity, forming the desert as well as the fertile land, without emphasizing human participation. God's work in controlling the universe and its forces are recognized by the Vision, but used only as background and proof of God's power in history. The Vision concentrates on God's need and use of servants in governing and in worship.

The Vision does make repeated, but isolated, forays into another territory. It portrays things in an ideal state, as presumably, if all things were in order, God would have them.

But the main thrust of the Vision's argument turns on realistic issues. It recognizes that neither Israel nor the nations are malleable clay in God's hands, but much more often they are resistant and rebellious. God's work, and his servants' work, is done under exactly such circumstances.

Here, however, the Vision notes that even within such a miserable and broken existence there are open windows of opportunity that could lead to a very different kind of world than that which they now experience. Things could and can be different. Some of these will be noted in the development of this section. God recognizes and calls his servants to recognize these moments in time which create the opportunity to make a real difference; for example, the call to reform worship in Jerusalem under Uzziah (1:18–20), Isaiah's challenge to Ahaz not to resist Aram and Israel (7:1–9), the opportunity opened by Ethiopian messengers to Hezekiah (chaps. 18–19), the opportunity given to Josiah (chap. 32), the opportunities in the rise of Cyrus (chaps. 44–45), of Darius (chap. 49), and of Artaxerxes (chap. 63), and others. The many factors of history move into certain constellations that offer opportunities for good for those governing as well as for the witnesses. These doors, however, only open for a moment. They must be entered decisively and quickly, or they will close again. The Vision says that God opens them and calls his chosen to enter them.

God's strategy for this new era included the arrangement of an entirely new political frame of reference (WBC 24:215). The empires of Assyria and Persia set the new stage on which the drama would be played. This closed certain doors and opened others. It was a wider stage. Israel was scattered throughout the empire. Canaan was now simply one province (or satrapy) in the great empire. The Vision insists that this was precisely God's strategy. Israel's political and national power are no longer factors or necessities. Its spiritual and religious distinctives are now all important. They will focus on Jerusalem as a worship center, a temple city. The emperor will help them build it. They will become the catalyst that enables worshipers from all peoples and nations to go there for instruction and worship. That is God's new strategy that Israel and the emperors are called to recognize and implement.

Readers in the twentieth century may recognize parallels. The political structures of the world have gone through tremendous changes. First, there were four centuries of intense colonization by the Western powers. This became a means of missionary activities of many kinds, and Christian teaching and preaching spread in a thin line throughout the world. Then, in the twentieth century that world collapsed. By mid century we entered the postcolonial era. God gave a small window in the movement of time for intensification of missionary effort, but of a very different kind, and the church has grown mightily in many parts of the "third world."

The writer of the Book of Isaiah would not hesitate to claim for God these great movements and changes in history, politics, society, and economics. He would challenge us to look for God's strategy that would bring people from all nations and tongues to worship at his feet and then challenge us to hear God's call to participate with him and with his governments in bringing this to reality. A window in time: "See the fields are even more white unto harvest." Time does not stand still nor is the window open forever.

Many persons need to work together to make this happen. God works with all of them. Some he encourages and enables. Some he restrains and redirects. Some he resists even to destruction. The Vision pictures persons who are called to govern in accordance with his strategy and pointed toward his goal. Some servants are called to govern and some are called to worship. Both serve God and his strategy. Both serve within the knowledge and understanding of God and his plans that he himself has provided.

The Book of Isaiah marks the passage of God's recognition of legitimate government in Canaan and over Israel from a Davidic king in Jerusalem (Uzziah) to a Persian emperor. The first moves reduced the Judean king's position to that of a vassal ruler of the city and its immediate environs while Assyrian armies destroyed Canaan's social and governmental structures. It took a century and a half and the help of a succeeding Babylonian Empire to accomplish that. The Judean ruler's life was preserved, but only as a king in exile living at the gracious table of the conqueror.

God's announced strategy for the world and for Israel had opposition. Judean kings resisted the changes, as undoubtedly did many of their subjects. Nevertheless, the symbol of principle rejection and rebellion to God's way was Babylon: Merodach Baladan's Babylon which rebelled against Assyria (chaps. 13, 14, 21, and 39) and the Babylon of Nabunaid (chaps. 46–47) which stood in the way of Cyrus.

Undaunted, God's strategy for rebuilding a shattered city and restoring a broken people took shape through the Persian emperors: Cyrus, Darius, and Artaxerxes. Each worked through a Judean leader: Sheshbazzar, Zerubbabel, Ezra, and Nehemiah. The task of restoration was finally accomplished with Persian money and protection and with Jewish leadership, priests, and a core of worshipers and workers.

The pattern was established for what we today call the separate powers of church and state. God is sovereign over both and is ultimately to be thanked for both. Neither can function without the other. The great buildings seem always to have required help from outside the people of God. Hiram of Tyre aided Solomon. The Persians aided Ezra and Nehemiah. Herod the Great built the beautiful temple in which Jesus worshiped. The Bible recognizes the divine sanction that gives legitimacy to their rule and their

Governing Servants and Their Service

obligation to create conditions in which the people of God can live and worship.

It is also clear that there are nations and rulers that do not have such sanction, whose very existence is in opposition to the divine will. Babylon is representative of this in Isaiah. Underlings and bureaucrats may also hinder God's people even when the emperor has given his blessing. Sometimes, however, the problems relating to society and government come from insiders, those among the people of God, the church, who oppose the plans of God, who neither understand nor agree to his ways. Every church group has its Judas.

In the Book of Isaiah the relative relations of the governing powers are presented throughout in terms of the Davidic heirs, the imperial rulers, and Babylon as the outside meddler and rebel. The pattern will be traced at three levels in the Vision. One might well organize the presentation differently with the same result. Governmental entities that affected Judah in the decade and a half that Ahaz reigned in Jerusalem (734–716 B.C.) are portrayed in the Book of Isaiah as "the house of David," the Assyrian kings, and the king of Babylon.

Ahaz: Eighth century B.C.

Ahaz and his son, presumably Hezekiah, represent "the house of David." He is called that in 7:2. The issue in these chapters is the survival of the throne. It is threatened, not by the Assyrian emperor, but by jealous and ambitious neighbors such as Edom in 587 B.C. (This is true throughout the period. The greatest threats also to Nehemiah came from Jerusalem's neighbors.) Ahaz is admonished to ignore Syria and Israel. He is to look instead at Assyria. That is the power to watch. That is where God's direction will come from.

Although Assyria's incursions will be devastating (7:17–8:8), the throne will survive. Ahaz will be able to place his heir on the throne, something neither Rezin nor the son of Remaliah will be able to do. This is God's sign (7:14–16). He is not finished with the Davidic dynasty. It will continue to be a keystone in his strategy and plan.

In developing this theme, the Book of Isaiah presents the most beautiful and powerful poetry concerning the Son of David in the Bible. This is, nonetheless, spoken about the heir to a throne threatened by ambitious and fractious neighbors, a country too weak to defend itself and soon to become the abject vassal of a foreign invader. That is just the point: the power and majesty of God will be revealed in this birth and birthright (9:6–7) and in the vision of the righteous king that the "Son of David" was meant and destined to be. This picture was and is true, not simply in the royal splendor of David's victories and Solomon's buildings, but also in the humility of vassalage and of the survival, after the throne no longer existed, in Sheshbezzar and Zerubabbel, even in a Nehemiah who shared no drop of David's blood.

The Book of Isaiah has seen in the Davidic house the purpose of God which reached far beyond the real throne and royal power. It represented God's reign in Jerusalem and over the land and the world. This kingdom of God is represented in the Davidic dynasty and the glory pictured there. It existed in its full glory more completely in the humble vassalage of Ahaz and his heir than in the ascending Assyrian emperor, although he, too, has a special role.

The child of sign and promise, given of God in Ahaz's lowest hour, is hailed as:

> Wonder Counselor,
> God-Hero
> Father of (the) Future
> Prince of Peace (9:5[6])

Such extravagant language was never applied to David or Solomon in the royal Psalms or elsewhere. Now it is given to the son born to Ahaz at the point when Judah ceased to have an independent existence. To that is added a promise and benediction:

> To the increase of rule
> and to peace (may there be) no end
> upon the throne of David
> and upon his kingdom.
> To establish it
> and to confirm it
> with justice and with righteousness
> from now and to the age.
> May the Zeal of Yahweh of Hosts
> do this! (9:6[7])

These are not just words spoken at a particular point in time. They are key passages in a book that is defining the way God works in a period of history in which the last remnants of David's proud empire are crumbling and in which the throne itself will disappear. The heirs will become royal guests (that is, prisoners) at the table of a foreign tyrant (Nebuchadnezzar) and will never again exercise royal rule in Jerusalem. In the face of this, the book proclaims the permanence and continuing significance of "the son of David" in such terms. And there is more:

> And a shoot shall go out from the stump of Jesse.
> A Branch from his roots will bear fruit.
> And the Spirit of Yahweh will rest on him:
> a spirit of wisdom and understanding,
> a spirit of counsel and wisdom,
> a spirit of knowledge, and fear, of Yahweh.
> His delight (will be) in the fear of Yahweh:
> who does not judge by what his eyes see
> nor make decisions by what his ears hear.
> When he judges poor people with righteousness,
> or when he gives fair decisions to the afflicted of
> the land,

or when he smites a land with the rod of his mouth,
with the breath of his lips he kills the wicked.
And this shall be, (when)
righteousness (is) the girdle of his loins
and faithfulness (is) the belt of his waist. (11:1-5)

The passage goes on to picture a day of no violence in all God's holy mountain. It closes with the words:

For the earth shall become full
of the knowledge of Yahweh
as waters (are) coverings for the sea. . . .
The root of Jesse,
who is standing
as a signal to the peoples,
to him nations will come seeking,
and his resting place will be glory. (11:9-10)

The Vision sees a fulfillment of the first verses in 61:1-3a, which begin "the spirit of the Lord of Hosts is on me." Here kingly grace and ministry is performed by someone lowly and very unroyal. Jesus could identify himself and his mission with this passage, and his compatriots could recognize Messianic meaning here. At the moment when power and worldly authority is being passed to the empires, the Book of Isaiah portrays the unction and ministry of the Davidic house in its most glorious and effusive form. The Gospels certainly agree.

The ascendant power of the Ahaz generation was the Assyrian Empire. After centuries of slow growth it burst upon the scene of the Mediterranean seaboard in the person of Tiglath Pileser, soon after the middle of the eighth century B.C. A major part of the Book of Isaiah is taken up with an exposition of its role in God's great strategy.

Its position as the most important nation of its day is hailed in 7:17. The thoroughness of its invasion and dominance is pictured like a plague or a flood in 7:18-8:18. The confusion as to what is going on and how the people of God should react to it is apparent in 8:9-22.

The rise of Assyria is linked to Israel's sin and God's judgment on her in 9:8-10:4. Assyria is pictured as the irresistible "rod" of God's anger in 10:5-11, and God's determination to keep control of this pagan nation is assured in 10:12-19.

God's work in history as explained to Jeremiah is both "to destroy and to build" (Jer 1:10). The Assyrians were God's destroyers who were succeeded in this by the Babylonians. God's strategy called for the power structures of Canaan to be dismantled (6:11-13), and the Assyrians were God's wrecking crew to that end—but they were more. They established a seat of power in Mesopotamia, with Canaan as its nearer colonies and with Egypt as its more distant dominion. This pattern continued with the Persians, although they revised and expanded their reign in Asia Minor and toward the east. Assyria was the first of God's imperial masters.

The picture would not be complete without the spoilers. Of course Aram and Israel (7:2) belong here, as do the Canaanite states (chaps. 15-22) in the next generation. The symbolic picture of resistance to God's established order, however, is Babylon. She and her king make the first of these symbolic appearances in the Ahaz section (chaps. 13-14; WBC 24:186-89).

God must deal with both Judah and Assyria as difficult, sometimes recalcitrant, servants, but Babylon was an enemy—a permanent enemy for God (13:19). She was such a symbol in the earliest civilizations, according to Genesis 1-9. In the latter reign of Ahaz a particular person usurped the throne in Babylon, taking it away from Assyria. His name was Merodach Baladan. He held the city for more than ten years and then returned to power briefly at the death of Sargon II.

Merodach Baladan's Babylon was a symbol of successful rebellion against Assyria. It was a tempting symbol that Ahaz refused to follow but to which Hezekiah succumbed twice (see below). It is no wonder that Babylon is seen in Scripture as a type of world resistance to God and that she seems to represent the Satanic Empire itself (Rev 14:8; 16:19; 17:5).

With these observations, God's strategy becomes clear and the direction of the book is established. In 14:22-27 God's strategy calls for the destruction of Babylon (vv 22-23) and establishes the temporary nature of his use of Assyria in Canaan (vv 24-27). 19:12-17 describes the expansion of imperial rule over Tyre and Egypt which placed the Mesopotamian land-based power in position to vie for control of Mediterranean shipping. This advantage set the stage for Persian ventures in that theater. 46:10-11 will use the word "strategy" to describe the role of Cyrus. The burden of government and power has been firmly placed in the emerging empires. They must do God's work of tearing down and building up. They are essential elements in the accomplishment of God's plan.

Hezekiah: Eighth century B.C.

The second cross section showing these elements of government and power is in the reign of Hezekiah. In it the Vision shows how difficult it was for the Davidic Dynasty to come to terms with its new status in God's economy. The section (chaps. 15-22; WBC 24:220-93) begins with emphasis on hopeful signs for the reign of Hezekiah. Then it pictures a marvelous window of opportunity to achieve political balance and a long peace in Palestine. Sargon II had just come to power in 715 B.C., the beginning of Hezekiah's reign. He had his hands full in many parts of the empire and necessarily relaxed his attention on Palestine. Egypt had four different Pharaohs claiming the throne at the same time. Chapters 18-19 picture the arrival in Jerusalem of a delegation from one of these claimants to Egypt's throne, the eventually victorious Ethiopians. They are apparently seeking help in establishing their power in Egypt, or at least the assurance that there would be no outside interference until it was accomplished.

Both Assyria and Egypt needed peace on their borders because of internal troubles. Both could have prospered with borders open to trade. These chapters in Isaiah suggest that a window of opportunity for establishing such order, permanence, and peace existed if Shabaka of Ethiopia and Sargon II of Assyria could have been brought to make common cause in the matter. Who could better act as intermediary than Hezekiah when Shabaka's messengers came to Jerusalem (chap. 18)? Chapter 19 suggests that Judah could have been elevated to a position beside Egypt and Assyria if such had been accomplished (19:23-25).

Instead of being a messenger of peace and an intermediary for building bridges for prosperity and blessing, which would have required daring in humility and subordination of prideful interests to the larger good, Hezekiah and his government brushed the delegation aside, wringing their hands in dismay that they would be drawn into Egyptian affairs. They apparently chose to follow Babylon's example and throw off the yoke of Assyria. So instead of the bright promise of 19:18-25, they had to feel the pain of the announcement of Babylon's fall in 21:9. Instead of helping cement the relation between God's winners, Shabaka and Sargon II, Hezekiah chose to seek support from the ill-fated rulers of lower Egypt's cities despite Isaiah's protests (chap. 20). Hezekiah was embarrassed and had to pay heavy tribute to the Assyrians.

Hezekiah neither acknowledged nor acquiesced to God's plan. Instead of the bright hopes of chapter 11 or of 19:19-25, his reign degenerated into a series of unsuccessful surrenders. The most humbling is pictured in chapters 22 and 36-39. Hezekiah led a rebellion of the Palestinian states against Assyria. Sargon II was dead. Merodach Baladan had seized Babylon again. Hezekiah hoped that this signaled a change in Assyrian fortunes; history and the Book of Isaiah know that this was not true (WBC 25:22-25). The Assyrian commander was better informed about God's plans than was Hezekiah (36:10). Yet even he overstated his case.

How often God must be placed in an awkward position by blind and rebellious servants as well as by arrogant and egotistic ones. To support the use of Assyria in his grand design and also implement his determination to spare Jerusalem, God arranges for both. The Assyrian had to withdraw, whether from illness to his troops or because of news from home (37:7, 36); Hezekiah barely escapes death and survives in a reduced state during the rest of his years (chap. 38).

Babylon's role is mentioned again (chap. 39). Merodach Baladan's messengers are shown all of the palace and Jerusalem's armaments (presumably before the humiliation and deprivations of chaps. 36–37; Merodach Baladan was driven out of Babylon before Sennacherib came to Jerusalem). Then Isaiah clearly shows that Babylon's place is not a positive but a totally negative one in God's plan. Hezekiah has submitted to her, and this will be fulfilled when his descendants will be exiled to Babylon to be prisoners in the king's house, and some will be made eunuchs to serve in the harem (39:6–7). The words were fulfilled in Jehoikim's removal to Babylon in 598 B.C. with his household (2 Kgs 24:10–16).

Persian emperors: Sixth–fifth centuries B.C.

The third cross section involves Persian emperors, Jewish subordinates, and Babylon (again) in chapters 40–66. The actual fall of Jerusalem and the beginning of the Exile are past. Isaiah is strangely silent about those events. God announces a new age and new rulers for the new period. The Book of Isaiah presents this in terms of three generations of ruling servants.

Cyrus. The first is presented in chapters 44–45. The conqueror is named: Cyrus of Media-Persia. He is anticipated in 41:2 where God claims credit for the approaching conqueror:

Who has aroused (one) from the east?
Whom salvation calls to its feet?

(Who) gives up nations before him
that he beats down kings?

Of him God says:

See my servant whom I confirm!
My chosen, in whom my soul delights! . . .
He does not shatter a bruised reed
nor put out a flickering wick.
(Yet) truly he does extend (the) verdict.
He does not fail. Nor is he discouraged
until he confirms (the) verdict in the land
and coastlands wait for his instruction.
(42:1, 3–4)

The specific mandate for Cyrus is spelled out:

I keep you and appoint you
to be a covenant (for) people,
to be a light (for) nations,
to open blind eyes,
to release a prisoner from a dungeon,
those who live in darkness from a prison-house.
(42:6b–7)

The reference to the exiled people is unmistakable. God's
way of helping Israel in her distress is to call on this bright
new conqueror and give him the mandate to assume control
of the land of Canaan and to bring release and salvation to
the exiles. Cyrus is introduced by name in 44:28 and linked
directly to the more specific assignment:

The one saying to Jerusalem: "Be inhabited!"
and to the towns of Judah: "Be built up!"
and to her ruins, "I will raise them!" (44:26)

God says this of himself. He supports "his servant" Cyrus (vv 26 and 28) who in turn says:

> to Jerusalem, "Be built!"
> and to (the) temple, "Be founded!" (v 28)

Then God concludes his appeal to Exilic Jews to recognize Cyrus:

> I myself have aroused him within my rights
> and I make all his ways straight.
> He builds my city
> and he sends out my exiles
> with neither bribe
> nor reward. (45:13)

Ezra 1:1-4 attributes this word to Jeremiah but confirms the decree of Cyrus for the people to return: "The Lord, the God of Heaven, has given me all the kingdoms of the earth and he has appointed me to build a temple for him at Jerusalem in Judah." So the change is made. The Persian emperor who by this time has control, at least in name, of all the larger areas, proclaims himself the patron of Jerusalem's temple. No one but a Davidic king had done that since Adoni-Zedek gave way to David. The new age provided for the foreign emperor to be recognized as God's servant with specific assignments which included the broader task of maintaining law and order throughout the empire, of releasing enslaved peoples, and of rebuilding Jerusalem and its temple. The concept is mind boggling! That history records that Cyrus and his successors actually did this is even more amazing.

Cyrus then commissioned a Jewish prince, Sheshbazzar (Ezra 1:8), to lead a delegation from Babylon to Jerusalem for the purpose of returning vessels taken by the Babylonians to the temple which they are to rebuild in Jerusalem. Ezra records fifty-four hundred articles of gold and silver that were committed to them (1:11). The Book of Isaiah is apparently picturing both this first expedition and Sheshbazzar:

> And now, Lord Yahweh,
> has sent me and his spirit. (48:16b)

and

> Move out from Babylon!
> Flee from Chaldea! . . .
> Say: "Yahweh has redeemed
> his servant Jacob!" (48:20a, c)

The Judean prince is in a subordinate and dependent position under the emperor, but he plays a significant role in the restoration and the work of rebuilding Jerusalem. The humbling process had gone from Ahaz (chap. 7) to Hezekiah (chaps. 22, 36–38), to Manasseh (2 Chron 33:11) to Josiah (whose humiliation led to his death; 2 Kgs 24:29; 2 Chron 35:20–24), to Jehoikim's captivity (2 Kgs 24:12–16), and finally to Zedekiah's mutilation and death (2 Kgs 25:4–7). Now Sheshbazzar assumes the humble role of representing Cyrus in the restoration of the city and the temple. This will be the pattern after the exile. The glory of an autonomous kingdom is no more. Nevertheless, the work of God is still carried out through this humble and sometimes humiliating role.

A third factor in the picture in Isaiah is played by Babylon (see "Excursus: Babylon," WBC 24:186–88). The powerful empire had disintegrated in the mid sixth century under Nabonidus and Belshazzar. The Book of Isaiah uses Babylon as the symbol of ultimate rebellion against God's plan in chapters 13–14, and 21, and as the seducer of Hezekiah's Jerusalem in chapter 39. Isaiah does not recognize expressly Nebuchadnezzar's Babylon as Assyria's successor in God's plan. Rather, in chapters 46–47, Babylon and its idols are pictured as humiliated. The gods are themselves taken captive. They are shown to be helpless and useless. Chapter 47 is a taunting song against Babylon.

Babylon is the ultimate symbol of humanity's pride (2:11–22 and 13:12) which must be judged by God. The Assyrians, too, had succumbed to the temptation of pride and ambition (10:5–54), but Babylon is always the prime symbol here (13:19; 14:11–15; 45:5). By the sixth century B.C. God had "finished all his work against Mount Zion and Jerusalem" (10:12). Babylon had been a rebel against God's strategy in that first phase (chaps. 13–14, 21). She is equally out of step now and cannot play any positive role.

The early readers of the Book of Isaiah in the late fifth century B.C. would have known, not only of Nabunidus's humiliating capitulation before the approach of Cyrus, but also of Xerxes' destruction of a rebellious Babylon in 480 B.C., although this is not noted explicitly in Isaiah. They must surely have looked on it as one more fulfillment of God's curse on Babylon in chapters 13–14.

The treatment of Babylon in the Book of Isaiah is a clear statement that not every conqueror, because of his success, is to be considered God's champion. He may, like Babylon, be God's archenemy—doomed for early destruction.

Darius. The second generation (chaps. 49–57) of the new order brings different players on stage, but the basic roles are the same. Darius has taken the place of Cyrus (WBC 25:180–81). Darius is recognized as the one chosen to succeed Cyrus in his God-appointed role as restorer of Jacob (49:5, cf. 42:7). He is honored as a "Light to the Nations" (49:6b).

The passage recognizes that Darius was an unlikely candidate for emperor (49:7b). He was in fact a military aide to Camlyses, not recognized as a possible heir to the throne. A rebellion killed Camlyses' brother, and a usurper claimed the throne. Most of the empire recognized the usurper, but the army, which had been with Camlyses in Egypt, and several of Darius's family stood firmly with him. Darius was able

Governing Servants and Their Service

to arrange the assassination of Gaumata, the usurper, and establish himself as ruler through a series of military campaigns. So, for a second time, a very unlikely candidate ascends the throne (49:7; 52:13-15), and the Book of Isaiah ascribes credit for it to God, who uses him as he had Cyrus to further his strategy.

Ezra 6 records an edict from Darius that supported the work to rebuild the temple in Jerusalem during the days of Haggai and Zechariah. This time a building was completed, services were held, and priests installed in the city. They celebrated Passover. The account in Ezra 6 credits Zerubbabel with the initiative in seeking aid from Darius. Zerubbabel, like Sheshbazzar, was a descendant of David (Ezra 3:2, 8; 4:2-3; 5:2). He was the leader most strenuously opposed by the governors of the neighboring provinces (Ezra 5:3-17). Inexplicably, Zerubbabel's name is missing in the account of the completion of the temple (Ezra 6:13-18).

The Book of Isaiah has a role for a Jewish leader in Jerusalem who is persecuted and oppressed (50:4-9) but who continues bravely and persistently in his work. The account continues in chapter 53. The people chant about someone who has apparently been executed, although they now recognize that he had been innocent of any crime. The chorus confesses their own guilt in the matter. Through the suffering and death of the one who was innocent, the entire group is declared guiltless.

> He was despised and rejected (by) men,
>> a man of pains
>>> who was visited by sickness.
> Like one hiding (his) face from us,
>> he was despised and we did not value him.
> Surely he bore our sickness!
>> and our pains—he carried them! . . .
> He was being wounded because of our rebellions.
> He was being bruised because of our wrongs.

The punishment for our wholeness was on him
and with his stripes comes healing for us.

(53:3-5)

The passage may be understood as drawing a parallel
between Darius and Zerubbabel (WBC 25:224-25, 227-29).
Darius is the unlikely servant who is finally recognized
and succeeds; Zerubbabel is the suffering martyr whose efforts and death finally bring imperial recognition and help
to Jerusalem.

In this section, too, there are enemies who initially
resist the rule of Darius and the leadership of Zerubbabel,
thus causing his death. They are identified in 49:26 as
"oppressors." They persecute the "teacher" in 50:6. They set
fires in 50:11. Some of these enemies may be identified as
the jealous leaders of neighboring provinces. Ezra identifies
some of these to be Tattenai, governor of the entire satrapy
of Trans-Euphrates, and Shettar-Bozenaiand, his aide (Ezra
5:3, 6). These, rather than Babylon, become the symbol for
rebellion and arrogance in this section. There is also the hint
that some of these enemies were actually among the Jews (see
esp. 56:1-13).

Artaxerxes. A third round in Isaiah's picture of post-Exilic
Judaism portrays the third of the Persian emperors who aided
in rebuilding Jerusalem: Artaxerxes. Almost a century afterward, he and Judah are called to a renewal of the purpose that
first accounted for the call and success of Cyrus.

Is not this the fast I would choose:
opening the bonds of wickedness,
undoing the bindings of a yoke,
and sending out the oppressed to be free?
You shall break every yoke! (58:6)

This echoes the words of 49:9:

Governing Servants and Their Service

to say to prisoners, "Go out,"
to those in darkness, "Appear."

spoken to God's servant (Darius) and those in 45:13:

He builds my city
and he sends out my exiles.

spoken to Cyrus. Artaxerxes is summoned to complete the work of Cyrus and Darius (chap. 60; WBC 24:290-95; and 61:4; WBC 25:298).

Ezra's return to Jerusalem (Ezra 7) and Nehemiah's work (the Book of Nehemiah) occur in the reign of Artaxerxes. The city walls were rebuilt, the temple organized, and priestly services established. The people were renewed in covenant with their God. This occurred because Artaxerxes renewed the edict to rebuild Jerusalem (Ezra 7:11-26) and sent both Ezra and Nehemiah to carry out these orders. This they did, and they completed the work. For the first time in a century and a half Jerusalem was a functioning city with an active temple.

Here the pattern is the same as in the first two rounds. God uses the pagan empire and also has his own persons to be the ones directly involved in the work. Here, too, there is opposition. Ezra 4:9 identifies Rehum, Shimshai, and other officials in Palestine among the non-Jewish population. Neh 2:19 and 4:1-3 identifies Sanballet the Horonite, Tobiah the Ammonite, and Geshem the Arab as active opponents. There were opponents among the Jews as well (Neh 5:1-19; 6:17).

The Book of Isaiah pictures a Jewish leader like Ezra in 61:1-3a:

The spirit of my Lord Yahweh is on me
because Yahweh has anointed me.
To bring good news to poor persons, he has sent me,
to bandage ones with broken hearts,
to proclaim liberty to captives
and an opening to those imprisoned,

> to proclaim the year of Yahweh's favor
> and our God's day of vengeance,
> to comfort all mourners,
> to assign (rights) to Zion's mourners.
>
> (61:1-3a)

All the emperor's favors for the city and the temple are not enough. A person with special spiritual and religious gifts is needed to bring the healing and renewal that God's people require. God is the ultimate one responsible for the government's provisions for the people as well as for the blessings through a spiritual leadership.

In this last section, enemies and opponents are still at work, but here they are located within Israel. Undoubtedly some of those who are judged for injustice in chapter 59 are neighboring leaders like those Nehemiah faced. The crucial listing in Isaiah 65–66, however, includes Israelites still addicted to pagan customs (65:2–7) who must be separated from the people of God (65:11–16) and finally be consigned to death (66:24).

There are also the faithful leaders of the people of God who try to exemplify and to effect the strategy of God for his people. They often work under extreme difficulty and at great risk and price. In Isaiah such were Ahaz (chaps. 7–14), Sheshbazzar (48:16–21), Zerubbabel (or whoever is represented in 50:4–9; 52:1–12), and Ezra (or whoever is represented in 61:1–3a). They were those who struggled to find ways to serve the purposes of God. They acted without power, in weakness, without glory, in humility and humiliation, without reward or apparent success. Nonetheless, the Book of Isaiah accords them the right to stand as predecessors of him who would serve God by taking up their mission (Luke 4:14–21) and by paying the same price for his service (Luke 22:37; Mark 10:45; Matt 20:28). He would predict another destruction of the temple (Mark 13:2), and he would speak of resurrection as a rebuilding of the temple in three days (John 2:19).

This pattern remained in effect for Judaism and early Christianity. Empire followed empire. The people of God in synagogue and church, first with the temple and later without it, learned to look to the government for essential services which they knew that God had provided, even though the rulers were pagans and nonbelievers. The people of God were thus free to do the things that only they could do.

6 WORSHIPING SERVANTS AND THEIR SERVICE

Israel's role in serving God

In the Bible "Israel" refers to the chosen people, heirs of Abraham, under the covenant of Sinai. They are the People of God. From them priests for the sanctuary are chosen. From among them rise the prophet-spokesmen for God and the teachers of the Torah. Their piety lies in conscious adherence to the instructions of God and in the sense of his presence among them. As the children of Abraham, and as Jacob and his sons, Israel is the reminder of God's promise. They lived with the hope of its fulfillment. Their experience in the wilderness teaches the idea of living in hope with the added factor of being a testimony to God's marvelous salvation from the land of bondage. Israel, as twelve tribes living in the land of Canaan, is a clear symbol of promises fulfilled: a great people, Abraham's descendants, living in God's land. The Book of Joshua tells the story. The books of Judges and 1 Samuel continue it.

Then Israel became a kingdom. Under David and Solomon the promise to Abraham reached its zenith of fulfillment. The whole land was under their control, and the people were numerous, the country prosperous. When the kingdom was divided Israel came to be the term used for the ten northern tribes. Their story is told in 1-2 Kings. The turbulent history of the Northern Kingdom lasted two hundred years (approximately 930-720 B.C.). During the last decades it was divided and often in civil strife before Assyria defeated it in 733 B.C. and finally incorporated it into its imperial structure in 720 B.C.

The Book of Isaiah picks up this identification of Israel during the reign of Jeroboam (1:1), the middle of the eighth century B.C. In chapters 1-14, the generations of Uzziah and Ahaz, "Israel" is the Northern Kingdom. The message of the book is that this kingdom of Israel is fated to be destroyed, a message parallel to that of 2 Kings. This is spelled out in 2:6-8 where Israel is not invited to worship in Jerusalem. In 5:24-25 the "woes" against her reach a climax of the Lord's anger because "they rejected the law of the Lord of Hosts and spurned the word of the Holy One of Israel." In 7:7-9 Ahaz is told that the Northern Kingdom with Aram will soon no longer exist. The terrible picture of its disintegration is recounted in 9:8-21. With these sections the identification of Israel as the Northern Kingdom comes to an end.

There are many indications, however, that God is not finished with the people of Israel. There is hope for a remnant (9:1, 10:20-21). In succeeding generations the term "Israel" is used sparingly. In 17:4-11 there is a description of Israel's role in God's future. Grief for the destruction is spelled out in 22:3-4. The sad picture of Israel's collapse is continued in the generation of Josiah (28:1-8). Only God's election grace offers any hope or dignity for them (28:9-18).

Yet God, who is identified as the Holy One of Israel, has no intention of letting the matter rest there. Chapter 40 introduces the generation when all Israel, including Judah and Jerusalem, has been humiliated. Most of them are in exile, scattered over Mesopotamia, with remnants in Egypt. This pitiful, straggly leftover from the period of autonomous kingship is addressed by God as "Israel."

He assures them that he is really the Creator of Heaven and Earth, the God of their fathers, even as they hear him in Babylon. He assures them that they are still, and always will be, heirs of his elective grace, the people of the promise, the potential people of the covenant. He calls them to be his servants. He has a job for them: to comfort, build up, and visit Jerusalem. Election is for service (see H. H. Rowley, *The Biblical Doctrine of Election*). Exilic and post-Exilic Israel is called anew to the service of God. Christians may well identify the church with this "Israel of God" (Gal 6:16) and the service to which it is called in the Book of Isaiah.

The exiles undoubtedly had a very low self-image. They had no power, no self-determination, no country of their own, no king. Nevertheless, God found them ideally located and situated to do the work he had in mind. Their immediate task was to encourage Jerusalem (40:1-2; for Jerusalem's role, see below). Babylonian Judaism was challenged to announce God's approach to Zion (40:9-10). Jews in Babylon remained a center of Jewish influence for centuries; the Talmud was shaped there in its famous academy. Jerusalem, however, became the center of Judaism until its destruction in A.D. 70. Babylon's, Alexandria's, and Asia Minor's roles were supportive in every way.

Babylonian Jewery is specifically endowed with the servant mantle in 41:8-24. They are called "descendants of Abraham," ones brought from the ends of the land to be told, "You are my servant; chosen and not rejected." They are assured of God's help and support, of being witnesses to God's miraculous revival of nature. They will overcome the basic problems of lack of knowledge and understanding that plagued their forefathers. They are called to "see and know, to consider and understand that the hand of the Lord has done this" (v 20). They have been "deaf and blind" (42:18-20), and therefore they have been "plundered and looted" (v 23). But now they should be able to know that God did this to them (vv 23-25). Unfortunately, they still do not understand (v 25b).

Worshiping Servants and Their Service

Beyond the trials by flood and fire (43:2), God points to redemption. He has called them by name. They belong to him (43:1, 4). They were "created for his glory, formed and made" for his purposes (v 7). Israel is to serve God by being a witness to his acts and calling (43:10). In a world filled with those who deny God's rights and his truth, Israel is called to witness on his behalf. They have been chosen to see, to ·know, and to believe, to understand that God is the source and author of all good and of their destiny (43:10, 12). The Christian church is heir to this calling and this service of witnessing to all the world (Matt 28:19–20; Acts 1:8). Israel is still called despite her forefathers' neglect of worship and their sin and rebellion (43:22–28). God is doing a new thing (43:18–20), and it is all focused on revival for his people (43:20c–21).

Israel is to share the service of God with the Persian emperor (see the next section), but his calling is "for the sake of Jacob, God's servant, Israel, God's chosen" (45:4). The emperor assumes part of the role that Israel formerly was supposed to fill, but his part is supportive only. The essentials of service continue with Israel, the people of God.

Israel, like the church at a later time, had its own ideas of what God wanted it to be. The Book of Isaiah notes this resistance (43:9–13 and afterward). It did not want to share its role with Cyrus or with worshipers from the nations. It arrogated to itself pretensions of worldly power and selfish ambition. It would not accept the fact that being separated for God meant renouncing all worldly things: power, wealth, and fame. Dependence on God meant renouncing self and its prerogatives. This it resisted, although God promised to provide all that was necessary through Cyrus, his chosen governor, through whom Israel would receive salvation and protection. This brings sharp words from God in 46:3–13. God's plan is fixed. He is determined to carry it out, but Israel's resistance is intolerable. One more time God appeals to Babylonian Israel in chapter 48 when the first expedition sets out for Jerusalem (48:16b, 20).

As the role of the emperor increases and as time stretches out in getting Jerusalem rebuilt, Israel complains that it is being neglected and its prerogatives are being overlooked (49:1-4). Indeed the Vision turns more attention to Jerusalem. Israel is confused and restless in its role. Chapter 58 reflects this confusion: "Why have we fasted, but you have not seen it?" (v 3). God's reply calls for a total life that conforms to his standards: "to loose the chains of injustice, . . . to set the oppressed free . . . to share your food with the hungry, provide shelter . . . clothe the naked" (vv 6-7) for their own kin as well as other human beings. They are admonished that rebuilding Jerusalem without building up their service to others in God's name is useless. Building Jerusalem must be accompanied by honoring the sabbath (v 13) for the cycle to be complete.

The message is still valid for the people of God. Erecting church buildings should be a means of reaching out to the needy, of furthering the causes of justice, and of worshiping God in his holy place on his holy day; "Then you will find your joy in the Lord."

Chapter 59 brings recognition that, in the new era as in the preceding one, the greatest hindrance to the fulfillment of God's promises lies in the sins of the people themselves (vv 2-8). Because of this their own justice and deliverance are far away, while they walk in more darkness than light (vv 9-15). So God's retribution is still necessary (vv 15b-19). Redemption is still offered "to those in Jacob who repent of their sins" (v 20). 54:17b has the term "servants of the Lord" in the plural for the first time in the Vision. The solidarity of the chosen people is no longer possible. The "heritage" will be received by some members of Israel but not by all. In chapter 55 the invitation to all who will to come is expressed. Here in chapter 59 those who may come are defined as "those in Jacob who repent of their sins" (v 20b).

63:7-13 recalls earlier days of Israel when people rebelled against the Lord even in the midst of their being saved. The reference is to the wilderness experiences after the Exodus.

Worshiping Servants and Their Service

There, too, God turned on the rebels (v 10). But they also remember the continued presence of "the Spirit of the Lord" who led the rest toward his promised land. Continued election to heritage in the promise is sure, but only to those in Israel who are willing and obedient, who repent and humble themselves before God. For them the new Jerusalem is open and ready.

The separation is spelled out in 65:13–16 following a description of latter-day pagans doing exactly what earlier generations had been condemned for doing. So the excommunication is complete. God speaks almost bitterly, "I revealed myself to those who did not ask for me; I was ready to be found by those who did not seek me" (65:1).

Servanthood for Israel was a sure selection through Abraham. At the same time, it required faith, obedience, and the will to belong to God and serve him. Post-Exilic Jews learned that not all of them were prepared to submit to God's plan or his requirements. They joined a long line in Israel, from Esau to the worshipers of the Golden Calf, to Saul and so on, who chose to exchange their heritage for something else. This way led to their own disinheritance and destruction. Even the new city bore silent witness to their rebellion and fate (66:24). This continued as a grim reminder that not all the children of Adam, or even of Abraham, want to be a believing, obedient, joyful part of the heritage God has prepared for his saints. Nevertheless, God is faithful, and the children of Abraham and the wider group of the children of Adam are issued an open invitation to the great celebration in the city of God (1:19; 2:3; 40:1–2; 55:1–7; 66:19–23).

Israel is the name of the people of God, chosen, called, and redeemed, who are responsive, obedient, and humble in their readiness to serve. Their service includes maintaining the place of worship, with open doors, holy for God, as well as witnessing to all peoples of the work, presence, and power of God, of his faithfulness, his holiness, his salvation, and his glory. They serve in supporting the cause of freedom and justice, of compassionate provision of housing, clothing, and food for the needy.

The Israel of God (Gal 6:16) and its service, which the Book of Isaiah portrays, is continued among the followers of Christ as his words echo the same invitation and definition of service. Still, the same sad truth follows the preaching of the Gospel: not all are prepared to receive it, believe it, and live it. Yet to those who believe the call the reward is sure.

The Book of Isaiah portrays the goal of God's strategy which has brought a new age into existence to be that of creating conditions in which genuine worship can take place. The old age and the old Jerusalem are condemned for having allowed worship to become totally depraved (1:10–15; 21–25). The only way God can accept them is through a total repentance (1:18–20) and through a process of purging and redemption (1:25–28; 4:4). The picture of the changed city portrays this goal (2:2–4).

The destructions portrayed in chapters 1–39 portray the process of purification and destruction. Chapters 40–66 sketch the emerging picture of the service of worship for this new age.

In the world

Israel is to be understood as God's servant in a primary sense. God's use of Cyrus as a governing servant does not displace Israel's essential calling. She is summoned to "comfort Jerusalem" (40:1–11). She is assured of her continued election (41:8–16), despite her blindness (42:18–21) and failure to recognize God's hand in her disasters (42:22–25). Israel is the centerpiece in God's great plan, the recipient of his redemption and care (43:1–7).

The purpose of Israel's existence and calling centers in her being God's witness: "You are my witnesses that I am God!" (43:12c). To fulfill that purpose Israel, scattered over the whole empire, is in a far stronger position than Israel in Palestine could ever have been.

God's condemnation of Israel in 1:2-3 was that Israel was a rebellious people "without knowledge or understanding." In 43:10-12 Exilic Israel is told:

> You are my witnesses,
>   expression of Yahweh
>   and of my servant, whom I have chosen,
> in order that you may come to know
>   and that you may confirm for me
>   and that you may understand that I am he.
> Before me, no god was formed,
>   and after me there is none.
> I, I myself am Yahweh
>   and apart from me (there is) no savior.
> I have announced (it), and I have saved and I
>   have let it be heard.
> And no one among you is a stranger (to
>   the facts).
> And you, yourselves, are my witnesses.
>   Expression of Yahweh!
>   I (am) God!

See also 44:8. She is called to overcome the very conditions that led to her forefathers' condemnation. The key words in verse 10 are "witnesses," "servants," "chosen," "know," "believe," and "understand." They have been central concepts through the entire book.

Israel's witness is to be directed first of all to its own people, to remind them of God's work in their history and to lead them to knowledge, faith, and understanding. Babylonian Jews did this to a remarkable extent for a millennium. Babylon's synagogues produced leaders and teachers. Its academy produced books, even the great Talmud that is so revered in Judaism. From Babylon, Ezra and many other teachers emerged.

The setting of verses 8-9 indicate that this witness will also apply to "the nations" as well. The setting probably has the nations of Canaan in view but is certainly not limited to them. The impact of Jewish synagogues on Gentile life in Babylon, Palestine, Egypt, and later throughout the Roman Empire was not inconsiderable. The Book of Isaiah expects "many peoples" to come to the new temple in Jerusalem (2:3) and lists those from Tarshish, Libya, Lydia, Tubal, Greece, and distant islands or coastlands among those who come to worship (66:19).

The New Testament testifies to the presence of such groups at Passover in Jerusalem (Acts 2:9), and Herod's temple had an entire section designated for the Gentiles. Jesus picks up the task which the Book of Isaiah saw as Israel's central calling and places it upon his disciples: "You shall be my witnesses in Jerusalem, and in all Judea and Samaria, and to the ends of the land [earth]" (Acts 1:8).

In Jerusalem's Temple

Servant Israel is also called to worship in Jerusalem's temple. Babylonian Jews were called to support efforts to rebuild and restore the city (40:2, 9, 11; 48:20-21), but the heart of Israel's calling relating to the city lies in worshiping there. The appeal in 1:7-20 is addressed in the plural to a gathered congregation. The issue is that their worship is unacceptable because of their behavior. Sacrifice not accompanied by a faithful life is unacceptable. A remedy, however, is available. They can purge themselves by changing their lifestyle:

> Cease doing evil!
>> Learn doing good!
> Seek justice!
>> Remedy oppression.
> Bring justice to the orphan!
> Plead the cause of the widow! (vv 16e-17)

Sin and guilt can be forgiven and cleansed "if you become willing and shall obey" (v 19a), but the ultimate fault is to

Worshiping Servants and Their Service

"refuse and continue obstinate" (v 20a). By the end of the book the people had experienced almost three centuries of the results of refusal and obstinacy.

The lesson in the form of a beautiful poetic parable in 5:1–7 is addressed to a group, and as individuals they are called to consider what options God has in this situation when:

> he waited for justice,
> behold bloodshed!
> For righteousness,
> behold a cry of distress! (5:7)

In chapter 40 individual exiles are summoned to "comfort Jerusalem." In chapter 48 those who comprise the first expedition to go to restore it are exhorted to leave Babylon.

In 54:17c, for the first time, "servants of Yahweh" appears in the plural. This verse speaks of their "heritage." Not the heritage of corporate Israel, but that of the group who gather for worship in Jerusalem. This is followed by the great unbounded invitation for any and all who "thirst" to come and "drink" (55:1). The open invitation to participate in Jerusalem's worship continues to the end of the book.

> Seek Yahweh while he may be found!
> Call him while he is near! (55:6)

The recognition that there is room for the repentant sinner, which was a feature of chapter 1, reverberates again:

> May the guilty forsake his way
> and the troublemaker his convictions.
> And may he turn to Yahweh that he may have
> compassion on him
> and to our God that he may multiply pardon.
> (55:7)

There is the clear recognition that God is different:

As (the) heavens are higher than land
so my ways are higher than your ways
and my convictions than your convictions.
(v 9)

But then God compares his blessings of rain for nature to his
blessing through his word in worship:

My word . . . does not return to me empty
unless it has done what I will
and succeeded in what I sent it (to do).
(v 11)

The protest that the foreigner and the eunuch could be left
out is answered by the assurance that they, too, have an
assured place:

To the eunuchs who keep my sabbaths
and who choose what I will
and who hold fast my covenant:
I shall give them
in my house and within my walls
hand and name.
Better than sons and daughters,
an age-long name I give to them,
which will not be cut off.
Foreigners who are joining themselves to Yahweh
to minister to him and worship the name of
Yahweh
to be his servants. (vv 4–6)

The words could not be more specific. "The servants of
Yahweh" will include all who choose to worship him in the
ways that he has stipulated: "keeping sabbath . . . and
holding fast my covenant" (v 6c). Then the temple is called
"a house of prayer for all peoples" (v 7c). The passage ends
with a clarification: God is still active in "gathering Israel's

outcasts," but there are so many "more than those already gathered" that he would welcome in his house (v 8).

The shaping of the new congregation does not proceed without problems. Judeans seek a "quick fix" for their problems by fasting and then complain that it has not brought immediate results (58:3). They still bring a mixture of human barbarism to their worship and do not see how incongruous it is:

> See! For strife and contention you fast,
>   and for hitting an adversary with a fist.
> You may not fast as (you have) today
>   (if you want) to make your voice heard on high.
>   (58:4)

With this the book returns to a central theme:

> Is not this the fast I would choose:
>   opening the bonds of wickedness
>   undoing the bindings of a yoke
>   and sending out the oppressed to be free?
> You (plural) shall break every yoke! (58:6)

We have noted above that this task of freeing the prisoners was the heart of the mandate given to the Persian emperors (42:7) and is picked up by his Jewish leaders in Jerusalem (61:1–3). In these verses (58:5–6) the members of the congregation are called to take up the task. They, too, are to be liberators. They cannot simply sit back and wait for the government to do God's work. As individuals they must participate:

> Is it (the fast God would choose) not sharing your
>   (singular) bread with the poor,
> and that you bring homeless poor persons
>   into your house?

When you see one naked and you cover him,
and you do not hide yourself from your own flesh.

(v 7)

Jesus echoes these words in his parable of the last judgment
(Matt 25:31-46).

In Isaiah's Vision the seekers move on through time as
well as space toward that exalted city on a high hill (2:2).
They seek the presence of God (2:3a), and they are prepared
to learn his ways through the Torah which is taught there
(2:3bc). These "ways" include the sense of social responsibility which is a requisite of true worship.

The tensions among the people and between the people
and God throughout the book and the journey come to a
climax in chapter 65. The near completion of the new city
forces God to deal promptly with those who continue in
rebellion (65:2). Some of these refuse to give up their pagan
rites (vv 3-5a, 11). Others hold on to a violent lifestyle that is
incompatible with worship in the new city (66:5b). Others
insist on traditional sacrificial worship without repentance
(66:3-4). These are judged:

Because I called, but you did not answer.
I spoke, but you did not listen.
So you did evil in my eyes
and you chose that in which I took no pleasure.

(65:12bc)

They are separated from God's servants (vv 13-15) and are
assigned to slaughter (vv 12a, 15b). The last verse in the book
is a reminder of their fate (66:24).

The worshipers in God's new city are a select group
who have been called of God, but they have also chosen to
seek him and are prepared to follow his way of worship
and life. The last passage in Isaiah calls on all these worshipers to:

Rejoice with Jerusalem . . .
all of you who love her. (66:10a)

Those who had been called to "comfort Jerusalem" (40:1)
may now be comforted by the Lord with Jerusalem (66:13)
when he comes "to gather all the nations . . . that they
may see his glory" (66:18). Some of these are sent out to tell
the nations that Jerusalem is open and to help them come by
all conceivable means of transport, and to bring offerings
and worship in the city (66:19–20). In this manner "all flesh
will come to worship before" God (66:23).

So the second type of worshiping "servant" is that of the
great congregation made up of all who seek God, who are
drawn to him, and who are willing and obedient.

Their worship is praise, thanksgiving, and communion. It
is listening to God's word, learning his instruction, living in
his ways. It includes doing God's work for the poor and
oppressed. It is a way of peace and is blessed by the Lord with
joy, comfort, and tranquility even under pressure and persecution. To learn from God in Zion means to learn the meaning of justice for everyone as the Torah (the Law) taught it.

Learn doing good!
Seek justice!
Remedy oppression!
Bring justice to the orphan!
Plead the case of the widow! (1:17)

In the crucible of judgment the picture of the just person
emerges:

Who among us can dwell indefinitely
(with) devouring fire? . . .
One walking (with) righteous acts,
one speaking upright things,
one despising gain from acts of oppression,
one shaking his hands so as not to hold a bribe,

one stopping his ears so as not to consent to bloodshed,
one shutting his eyes so as not to favor evil,
only that one will dwell in the heights. (33:14c–16a)

The one called of God defined his mission:

To bring good news to poor persons, he has sent me,
to bandage one with broken hearts,
to proclaim liberty to captives . . .
to proclaim the year of Yahweh's favor,
and our God's day of vengeance,
to comfort all mourners. (61:1b–3a)

This moves well beyond the Law's definitions but is within
the kind of worship that God wants.

To worship in Zion pointed the way to a nonviolent
world, to peace as God's will for all who would worship him.
There "the wolf and the lamb will feed together" (11:6a):

They will do no harm—
they will not destroy
in all the mount of my holiness! (11:9a)

The result of righteousness is peace . . .
quietness and trust for an age,
so that people dwell in peaceful homes
in secure dwellings
and in quiet resting places. (32:17–18)

Indeed you will go out in joy
and be led out in peace.
The mountains and the hills break out before you
in singing,
and all the trees of the field clap their hands. (55:12)

Jesus echoes the theme: "Blessed are the peacemakers, for
they shall be called the sons of God" (Matt 5:9).

To worship God in Zion means to learn humility and meekness. Only those who are "contrite" and "humble" can experience the presence of God in its fullness. "The willing and the obedient" experience God's blessings (1:19). The humble and the needy will rejoice and exult in God (29:10). "The one who takes refuge in (God) will possess the land" (57:13b). God welcomes "the contrite and lowly in spirit" to his high and holy place to dwell with him (57:15), and in the new temple God says:

> I pay attention to this (one):
> to a humble and contrite spirit
> who trembles at my word. (66:2b)

Jesus said, "Blessed are the meek, for they shall inherit the earth" (Matt 5:5).

To worship God in Zion is to recognize the fruits of dedicated service in suffering and even through death:

> My Lord Yahweh has assigned me
> a student's tongue
> to know how to sustain a weary one (with) a word. . . .
> I gave my back to ones who beat me
> and my cheeks to those who plucked them bare.
> (50:4, 6a)

> Surely he bore our sickness!
> and our pains—he carried them! (53:4)

> Yahweh laid on him
> the iniquity of us all. (53:6b)

Even among the celebrants were some who had been disowned for their faith (66:5). Jesus said, "Blessed are those who are persecuted because of righteousness, for theirs is the kingdom of heaven" (Matt 5:10). To worship God in Zion is to experience how God prepared the way for all who yearn for his presence and who are willing to do his will.

Ahaz faced seemingly impossible opposition, but God showed him a way if he would confirm himself in God (chap. 7; WBC 24:94). Manasseh's generation faced a totally desolate land in which death was everywhere, but God by sovereign decree "swallowed up death" (25:8; WBC 24:332-33). Israel in exile seemed to face impossible odds, but God called them to remember that, as creator of the world, he had assets available beyond their ability to imagine (chap. 40; WBC 25:93). He used pagan emperors and their imperial resources to prepare a temple for believers to assemble to worship him (chaps. 60 and 66). Jesus says, "Blessed are those who hunger and thirst for righteousness, for they shall be filled" (Matt 5:6) and "Whoever seeks shall find" (Matt 7:7).

To worship in Zion is to be alive and to live as God would wish. The promise of life is inherent in the emphasis on "sons" in chapters 7-9 for Ahaz and for Isaiah (WBC 24:84). Hezekiah came to appreciate how precious life is in his psalm celebrating his gift of continued life:

> The living! (Only) the living!
> He it is who thanks you
> as I do today. (38:19)

God's control of death is vital to his people in the dark days of chapters 24-25. (See esp. 25:7 and 26:19; WBC 24:343.)

To worship in Zion is to learn to be the servant of the Lord that Israel was called and destined to be. In contrast to the role of ruler that Cyrus is called to fill, Israel is to return to the role of worship and holy living that began at Sinai. This role is secure for her even in exile (41:9), and it is for this purpose that he redeems her (WBC 25:106). Israel's experience points to this end (43:27-44:2). It is for Israel to learn how to include the foreigner and the banned (56:6-7) and to worship after God's fashion through service to others (58:5-14). Jesus fit this pattern when he said: "Whoever wants to be great among you must be your servant. . . . For even the Son of man did not come to be served, but to serve and to give his life as a ransom for many" (Mark 10:43, 45).

To worship God in Zion is to know God's grace and restoration beyond judgment:

Indeed you have been angry with me.
May your anger turn
that you may comfort me. (12:1b)

Indeed when your judgments belong to the land
they teach righteousness to the world's inhabitants.
(26:9b)

For it was not a discerning people.
Therefore he had no compassion on them. . . .
But it will be in that day . . .
you, yourselves, will be gathered. (27:11b-12)

Do you not know? . . .
Yahweh is a God of the long view. . . .
He does not faint!
He does not grow weary! . . .
(Yet he it is who is) giving power to the faint
and he multiplies strength to one with no
might. . . .
Those waiting on Yahweh
will renew strength.
They will rise (on) wings like eagles.
They will run, but not tire.
They will walk, but not faint. (40:28-31)

To worship God in Zion is to know God's ultimate triumph over evil:

In that day
Yahweh with his sword will decide the fate of
the hard, great, and strong one,
of Leviathan, a fleeing serpent,

Leviathan, a twisting snake.
And he will kill the monster which is in the sea.

(27:1)

To worship God in Zion is to know "wonder after wonder" and know they are true and real.

Therefore, see me again
doing wonders for this people,
the wonder and a wonder! (29:14a)

Remember . . . I am God!
There is no other! . . .
Announcing end from beginning. . . .
Indeed, I have spoken. Indeed, I bring it to pass.
I have planned (it)! Indeed, I do it! (46:9–11)

To worship God in Zion is to experience the spirit poured
from on high; that is, a judgment:

Until spirit is poured upon us from above.

(32:15)

I pour my spirit on your seed
and my blessing on your offspring. (44:4b)

and a leader who says: "And now, Lord Yahweh has sent me
and his spirit!" (48:16) and "the spirit of my Lord Yahweh is
on me" (61:1). Jesus spoke in terms like these (Luke 4:21),
and Peter at Pentecost claimed the fulfillment of the out-
pouring of God's spirit (Acts 2:16).

To worship God in Zion is for the blind to see and the
deaf to hear. It is to know the lifting of the curse spoken in
6:10, in which deliverance was promised:

The deaf hear in that day
words (read from) a scroll.

After gloom and darkness
blind eyes will see. (29:18)

If the eyes of those who see should look
and the ears of those who hear should hearken.
(32:3)

Then blind eyes are opened
and a deaf ear is cleared. (35:5)

And you shall see and your heart will rejoice.
(66:14)

Jesus, too, spoke of worship as "seeing and hearing" when he was healing a blind beggar (Luke 13:42); "He who has ears to hear, let him hear it" (Luke 14:35b). To worship in Zion, however, is to recognize that this is a privilege that many do not want and will not tolerate: "A wicked one shown mercy does not learn righteousness" (26:10).

Worship in Zion is restricted to those who will do it in God's way (65:1-7, 11-12). Those who refuse to do it that way may not enter (65:1-16) and have only death as their fate (66:24). As God is forced by human rebellion and recalcitrance to recognize that not everyone wants to worship in Zion, so must those who do come recognize this sad and bitter truth: "There can be no peace for the adversaries" (48:22; 57:20-21). Worship in the new city is open to all who seek God and want to submit to his instruction. Sadly, there are many who do not want this.

In quietness and solitude

There is a third kind of worshiper which the Vision of Isaiah portrays. This kind is pictured as the most valued of all by the Lord. This one approaches God alone in quietude to share his presence simply.

Ahaz is offered such a communion in the midst of his busy life by the prophet Isaiah in chapter 7. He is told:

"Take hold of yourself and be calm. Do not be afraid. . . ."
If you will not believe,
    certainly you cannot be confirmed. (7:4a, 9b)

This remains one of the best descriptions of personal faith to be found anywhere. To make oneself firm toward God allows God to confirm one in his purpose and in his care. (See "Excursus: The Risk of Faith" WBC 24:94–95.)

Isaiah retreats into privacy from the tempestuous public ministry saying, "I will wait for Yahweh who is hiding his face from the house of Jacob and will hope for him" (8:17). Waiting and hoping are essential elements of this quiet faith that God treasures, as their repeated use in the Psalms show. Yet it is in the passages near the end of Isaiah, when the tensions and failures of the people are so evident, where God sighs his appreciation of the simple believing worshiper most poignantly.

God's measured movements toward accomplishing his goals call for patient waiting. When so many want to act impatiently and impetuously to force God's hand, he announces his goal and defines the one who can share it.

See me laying a stone in Zion.
    A tested stone.
    A corner (stone) of value.
    A foundation (well) founded.
He who believes will not be in haste. (28:16)

This may well call for continuation in faith when there is no understanding of the ways of God. The Book of Isaiah recognized this: "Strange is his work. . . . Alien is his service" (28:21b). That God could pronounce harsh and binding judgment on his own people (6:9–13) and carry it out was indeed strange and alien. That God would call on a heathen king to effect his salvation for his people was stranger still (45:15).

So faith had to include patience in waiting for God to reveal his plan and effect his salvation. It had been so for

Abraham. It had to be so for believers during the span of history that Isaiah covers. It still is so today.

When the signs of God's judgment are so evident that terror seizes everyone, the question is asked, "Who among us can dwell indefinitely (with) devouring fire?" (33:14). The situation is like that addressed in Habakkuk who asks "How long, O Lord?" in 1:1, to be answered, "The righteous by his faith will live" (3:2). The answer in Isaiah is also of an individual:

> One walking (with) righteous acts,
>   one speaking upright things,
> one despising gain from acts of oppression,
>   one shaking his hands so as not to hold a bribe,
> one stopping his ears so as not to consent to bloodshed,
>   one shutting his eyes so as not to favor evil,
> only that one dwells in the heights.
>   Rock fortresses (will be) his defense.
> His bread will be provided.
> His water will be assured. (33:15–16)

The passage goes on to envision for this person a king and a city where God reigns in supreme peace.

What separates a person from God is not vulnerability to his holy fire, but rather incompatibility in terms of character and commitment. It is not because a person is human that the fire is to be feared but because a person is a sinner who cannot stand in God's presence (WBC 24:427–28).

As the pressures of international violence close in on Judah in chapter 30 and its leaders have still not learned to accept a passive role in international politics so as to be able to assume a new role as God's spiritual representatives to the world, God calls again for one among them who is capable of turning inward in faith, of resting on God's grace and promises:

> In returning and rest you could be saved.
>   In quietness and trust
>   could your heroism consist. . . .

Surely, Yahweh waits to be gracious to you.
Surely, he rises up to show you mercy,
for Yahweh is a God of justice.
Blessed are all who wait for him! (30:15b, 18)

This is indeed a very different kind of heroism, the heroism of waiting on the Lord, of meeting God's patient waiting with hope and faith that is willing to wait. This is a major theme in Isaiah (WBC 24:397). The tragedy for ancient Israel and so often for us lies in our insistence on trying to fashion our own salvation. We fail again and again. The solution is to learn to let God show his grace, to learn to wait. Such a person waits and hopes for that temple "not made with hands" (Heb 9:11) which is pictured here for the oppressed Judean where "Yahweh (will be) our king. He will be our Savior" (33:22).

As the Vision nears the accomplishment of God's goal, one might expect the light to break and all tensions to be released, but as the restoration of the City and its temple draws near, the more the tension grows and the more difficult it becomes to be God's person. Chapter 57 portrays a scene of chaos, paganism, and unbelief among God's people. At the end, however, God affirms that the position of the faithful is rock solid and invulnerable:

The one who takes refuge in me will possess land.
He will inherit my holy mountain. (57:13)

Among all those who had given up on waiting for God to reward his own, who had turned to pagan, violent, and unethical ways to assure their living and their possessions, God affirms those who simply find their peace in him. Final peace and ultimate inheritance belong to those "who take refuge" in God (WBC 24:160).

God's goals and strategy are built around a simple truth:

Thus says one high and lifted up,
Dweller Forever whose name is Holy:

I dwell in the high and holy place
with one contrite and lowly of spirit
to revive the spirit of humble ones
and to revive the heart of those practicing contrition.
(57:15)

No matter how high one's view of God is (as in 57:15a) or how exalted one's picture of the position of the believer is (as in verse 15bc), the description of the one privileged to share that spot is of humility and contrition. The essential attribute of true faith is humility. And the common purpose of God and those who share the exalted and holy tryst is to revive those who are humble and contrite, those awesome "meek who will inherit the earth" whom Jesus spoke of (Matt 5:5).

God is very selective about the ones who are invited to share his presence, to come to the inmost part of his temple. Those who are "adversaries," who oppose his strategy and plan are excluded (57:21). The proud and the haughty, the "successful" and knowledgeable, are not included.

God offers a place in his house, the temple, in his presence, to the contrite, the humble, and the lowly in spirit. There is no other requirement, none of race or creed. Those humble souls who would seek God are welcomed with a promise of spiritual renewal. How like God to offer a spot in his highest place to persons who have the lowliest stations in life! Jesus pictures the beggar Lazarus in the bosom of Abraham (Luke 16:20–21) and tells the religious leaders that the lowliest outcasts of society will enter the kingdom of heaven before them (WBC 25:164).

God waited in expectation for Israel (5:2, 4, 7). The Prophet Isaiah waited in hope (8:17). When God's redemption is revealed, those redeemed will say, "We waited for him and he saved us" (25:9). The righteous say, "We wait for you" (33:2). In the new age, "Those who wait for the Lord will renew strength" (41:31). God says, "Those who wait for me will not be disappointed" (49:23); "Coastlands look toward me and hope for my arm" (51:5b).

Sometimes the waiting can include persecution as in 50:4–10 or even martyrdom as in chapter 53. Hope, nevertheless, still rests in God:

The one who takes refuge in me will possess land.
He will inherit my holy mountain. (57:13b)

Sometimes the waiting is unrewarded:

We wait for justice, but there is none.
For salvation, but it remains far from us.
(59:11b)

But the prayer of the faithful confesses:

From (that) age (until now) no one has heard of—
no one has attended—
no eye has seen
any God except you
who works for one who waits for him.
(64:45)

For those who wait, the great experience of fulfillment awaits in the new heaven and the new earth as the doors of the temple open for worshipers from all the known world (65:17–66:24).

The focus of the Vision is on those who were willing in faith to listen to God and leave the fulfillment of the Vision to him. Luke tells of two such Israelites "waiting for the consolation of Israel," Simeon and Anna (Luke 2:25–38), who were "looking forward to the redemption of Jerusalem" and were ready to greet the new-born Jesus.

This work of "reviving the humble" is spelled out in detail:

Worshiping Servants and Their Service

Is not this the fast I would choose:
    opening the bonds of wickedness,
    undoing the bindings of a yoke,
    and sending out the oppressed to be free?
You shall break every yoke! (58:6)

It includes the struggle to help everyone be free and to gain justice for all. The instructions, however, go beyond these broad movements:

Is it not sharing your (sg) bread with the poor,
    and that you (sg) bring homeless poor persons
        into the house?
When you (sg) see one naked and you cover him,
    and you (sg) do not hide your self from your own flesh,
then your (sg) light will break out like the dawn
    and your (sg) healing will spring up in a hurry.
                                        (58:7–8a)

The singular address is indicated, but its application is distributed among several. The first promise of light and healing is appropriate for Judah. The second address promises "legitimacy" or "righteousness," which usually in Isaiah refers to the promise to the Persian ruler (WBC 25:133–35):

Your (sg) legitimacy will walk before you.
    Yahweh's glory will be your rearguard. (58:8b)

And it is then addressed to the humble worshipers:

Then you (sg) may call
    and Yahweh will answer.
You may cry out
    and he will say, "I am here." (58:9a, b)

The tasks of social sensitivity and action are passed around to all the participants: those in government, the people of

God, and the person who seeks God's presence and blessing. The promise of God's blessing and help are repeated for all of these (58:10-14):

> when you (sg) pour out yourself for a hungry one
> and you satisfy an afflicted person. (58:10a)

The doing of helpful acts for the needy is paired with keeping the Sabbath (58:13) as requisites for anyone to:

> delight in Yahweh. . . .
> ride on the heights of the land
> and . . . eat from the heritage of Jacob.
> (58:14)

The picture of God's attention to the humble person of prayer reaches its height in 66:2b. God's new creation of heaven and earth has just been described, a society without the shortcomings of the current order. God puts the temple project in perspective by comparing it to the great universe in which he dwells:

> The heavens are my throne
> and the land is my footstool. . . .
> My own hand has made all these. (66:1a, 2a)

Then he utters the highest peak of all his relations:

> I pay attention to this (one):
> to a humble and contrite spirit
> who trembles at my word. (66:2b)

Not the priests with their sacrifices, not the mighty with their ostentatious offerings, but the "humble and contrite spirit."

With that, one is reminded of all the quiet, simple, faithful believers in congregations of Israelites or Christians who fill that description. The Old Testament pictures Hannah (1 Sam 1:1–2:11). The New Testament honors Mary in the same way. Her words become the example of humble response to God (Luke 1:38, 46–47). These are the humble and contrite, the lowly of spirit who tremble at God's word, who wait patiently, who hope and believe and pray. They share the inner circle around the Lord. Their devotion constitutes the bright spots in time which is otherwise often spoiled by violence, rebellion, and back talk.

CONCLUSION

The Vision of Isaiah sees a convergence of the work of many and different servants at two very practical points. One of them involves the restoration of Jerusalem and its worship. Servants Israel, Cyrus, and various individuals are involved in that project in different but interrelated ways. Like the task of building and sustaining the institutional church today, the building of Jerusalem needed support from all sides.

Government plays a role, too. It is not the church, nor should it dominate it, but it is responsible for creating a favorable climate of peace and order in which the church can survive. It supplies necessary aid. In the United States it has tax-free status and encourages charitable giving. In a society where all property is owned or controlled by the government it must assign the property and approve the funding if any building takes place. The latter situation existed at the time Isaiah was written.

The primary responsibility, however, must rest with the congregation of believing, committed, and called people of God. Coming from near and far, they must be those who encourage and support the building and the enterprise, as Israel in exile was called to do in Isaiah.

Then there are the leaders who bridge the gap between the elect and the government. They organize and exhort the former, plead and work with the latter, while fending off enemies on all sides, to bring the project to successful completion or to keep the organism alive and functioning afterward. Like Sheshbazzar, Zerubbabel, Ezra, and Nehemiah, these church leaders exhort, organize, plead, pray, and work to make the restored Jerusalem all that it is supposed to be as the city of God.

All of this stands in the service of that high moment when the seekers climb the hill to assemble in the presence of God. Then the praises rise, the choirs sing, the people pray, and the glory cloud descends on the holy place. Then the mighty congregation of people from all nations experiences the fruit of all that labor and devotion. The Holy City is populated with pilgrims and with God's presence.

Yet the Book of Isaiah records one precious insight beyond that. God's pleasure is at its peak in the individual tryst with each humble and contrite soul that seeks him out on Jerusalem's high and holy mountain (or anywhere else). In the simple and lowly attitude of devotion and prayer God's creation achieves the goal for which it was intended.

Those are the many facets that are summed up in the theme of building and restoring Jerusalem. There is a second focus that goes along with that and also involves all of God's servants. It speaks of service on God's behalf for the needy and oppressed peoples.

Israel thought of itself as imprisoned and poor, but it, too, was entrusted with support and succor for the needy. Cyrus was called to free the imprisoned and to restore the fallen. His successors in office were given parallel instructions which included aid to Israel as well. Israel's leaders were called to announce and to exhort her to fulfill the role of aiding the needy and comforting the mourners. And the humble devotee was called beyond the exercise of spiritual devotion to acts of charity and love.

With these two emphases, the building of the church and the work of charity to all in need, Isaiah speaks to us with a clear voice that is echoed in the Gospels. Love God, build his city, and care for his beloved poor. For those who wait, the great experience of fulfillment awaits in the new heaven and the new earth as the doors of the temple open for worshipers from all the known world (65:17–66:24).

APPENDIX A

The New Testament's use of Isaiah

Nestle's Greek New Testament contains an index of New Testament quotations and allusions to Old Testament texts. It shows (pp. 665–67) that Isaiah has had an unusually great influence on the New Testament: 194 New Testament passages contain allusions to verses from 54 of Isaiah's 66 chapters. The references are particularly frequent in Matthew, Luke/Acts, Romans, Hebrews, and Revelation.

Three passages are quoted three times each. Isa 6:9, 10 ("Dull the heart of this people! Make its ears heavy and shut its eyes") is quoted in Matt 13:14–15, John 12:4, and Acts 28:26–27. It emphasizes the New Testament perception that Isaiah's ministry in a hostile and insensitive environment was mirrored in the chilly reception given Jesus and the early Christians.

Isa 40:3 (in the way the Septuagint translated it: "A voice crying in the wilderness") is quoted in Matt 3:3, Mark 1:3, and John 1:23, while Luke 3:4–6 alludes to it. The parallel between the "bearer of good tidings" to an unbelieving, exilic community and John the Baptist is clearly drawn.

Isa 56:7 ("For my house is to be called a house of prayer for all peoples") is quoted in Matt 21:13, Mark 11:17, and Luke 19:46. The parallel between Isaiah's view that the temple should be a place for singing, prayerful worship, and pilgrimage (in contrast to priestly sacrifice and liturgy) and Jesus' view of worship without sacrifice or priest is clear.

Two passages are quoted twice. Isa 29:13 ("Because this people approaches me with its mouth . . . while its heart is far from me") is quoted in Matt 15:8-9 and Mark 7:6-7, while Col 2:22 alludes to it. 1 Cor 2:22 quotes verse 14. Isa 53:1 ("Who believed our report?") is quoted in 1 John 12:38 and Rom 10:16. The New Testament writers empathize with the basic climate of unbelief to which Isaiah testifies.

At key points in Matthew's Gospel, Isaiah supplies just the right quotation. Isa 7:14 (in the Septuagint: "Behold, a virgin shall conceive and bear a son") fits Matt 1:23. Similarly, Isa 53:4 ("Surely he bore our sickness") provides the comment in Matt 8:16 on Jesus' ministry of healing and casting out demons.

Matthew quotes from Isaiah fifteen times. Five of these are in the birth narratives. In 4:15-16, Jesus' ministry in Galilee recalls Isa 8:23-9:1, which begins with references to Zebulun and the Galilee of the Nations and continues "the people walking in the dark see a great light."

The Beatitudes in Matt 5:3-4 recall Isa 61:3 in references to ministry to the poor and the mourners. As noted above, Jesus' ministry to those possessed by demons recalls Isa 53:4 ("Surely he bore our sickness").

Matt 12:18-21 reveals Jesus' messianic identity to readers by quoting Isa 42:1-4 ("See my servant whom I confirm"). Jesus explains his use of parables by quoting Isa 6:9-10 ("Dull the heart of this people"). Jesus cites the shallow faith of the people in Matt 15:7-9 by quoting Isa 29:11 ("Because this people approaches me with its mouth . . . while their heart is far from me").

Matthew's description of Jesus' triumphal entry into Jerusalem quotes Isaiah twice. In 21:5 his quotation mixes words from Isa 62:11 with those of Zech 9:9 ("Say to the daughter of Zion—see your king [Isaiah has 'your savior'] comes to you"). Matt 21:13 quotes Isa 56:7 in justification for the cleansing of the Temple: "For my house shall be called a house of prayer for all peoples."

The use of Isaiah is remarkable in the New Testament for its ubiquitous appearance, strongest in Romans and Matthew but virtually everywhere else. The Revelation of John never quotes Isaiah but reflects its poetic wording in almost every chapter.

Another remarkable feature of the New Testament's quotations and allusions is that they are drawn from so much of the Book of Isaiah: 54 of the 66 chapters. The Apostles and apparently many Jews of that time knew the entire book well enough for it to be a part of their thought, the heritage that shaped their views on everything. It was not the plot, the outline, or the thrust of the book which captured their interest and imagination. Quotable quotes stuck in their minds and gave words to their thoughts.

APPENDIX B

Isaiah in Handel's Messiah

Many in England and in the United States are probably more familiar with Isaiah's words sung in George F. Handel's *Messiah* than in any other setting. Charles Jennens was Handel's librettist. He arranged the oratorio in three parts: the birth of Messiah, the crucifixion, and the resurrection. Texts from Isaiah play prominent parts in the first two parts, often following the order of the Anglican Book of Common Prayer.

The first part uses Luke's account of Jesus' birth (Luke 2:8–14) to recite the basic narrative. He introduces it with twelve recitatives and choruses. Four of these use words from Isa 40:1–5, 9: "Comfort Ye," "Every Valley," "And the Glory of the Lord," and "O, Thou that Tellest Good Tidings to Zion." Four others use Isa 9:1–6: "Behold Darkness," "The People that Walked in Darkness," "For unto Us a Child Is Born," while "O Thou that Tellest Good Tidings" credits 9:1 as well as 40:9. Isa 7:14 makes the crucial announcement "A Virgin Shall Conceive and Bear a Son." Isa 35:5–6 provides the words for "The Eyes of the Blind Shall Be Opened," and

40:11 the words for "He Shall Feed His Flock Like a Shepherd." The blending of prophetic and New Testament texts creates a tapestry of incomparable beauty which blurs the distinction between the original and applied meanings of the texts.

Isa 7:14 had already been appropriated by Matthew while 9:1, 6 are alluded to in Luke 1:32–33, 79. Isa 40:3 plays a role in Matthew's call of John the Baptist (3:3), as in Luke's account (3:4–6) as well as in Luke's recounting of the words of Simeon (2:30). The New Testament accounts, however, do not use Isaiah 40 so intensely and effectively to place the birth of Jesus as a central event in God's action as does the *Messiah*.

In Part 2 (The Crucifixion), Isa 53:1–6 tells the central story: "He was Despised," "Surely He has Borne Our Griefs," "And with His Stripes We Are Healed," "All We Like Sheep Have Gone Astray," "He Was Cut Off from the Land of the Living." John 1:29 ("Behold the Lamb of God") had opened the section, and other words are taken from Psalms 2, 22, and 68. Isa 52:7 ("How Beautiful") is a part of the exultation that leads up to the Hallelujah Chorus.

No Isaiah texts appear in Part 3 (The Resurrection). Only Job 19:22–26 introduces the section with "I Know that My Redeemer Liveth." The other texts are taken appropriately from 1 Cor 15:22–22, 52–57 and Rom 5:12–12; 8:31–34.

Isaiah's wonderful poetry fits the oratorio perfectly. Its powerful genre of poetic drama within an imaginative frame of reference enables it to awaken emotion and imagination to the wonder and power of God at work in redemption. Handel's music adds a new and supportive dimension to it.

FOR FURTHER READING
IN RECENT LITERATURE

Elizabeth Achtemeier. *The Community and Message of Isaiah 56–66.* Minneapolis: Augsburg, 1982.

Christopher R. Seitz, ed. *Reading and Preaching the Book of Isaiah.* Philadelphia: Fortress Press, 1988.

John D. W. Watts. *Isaiah 1–33.* Word Biblical Commentary 24. Waco, Tex.: Word Books, 1985.

———. *Isaiah 34–66.* Word Biblical Commentary 25. Waco, Tex.: Word Books, 1987.

INDEX OF SCRIPTURES

1:19-20	16, 42, 50	10	52	24:22	52
1:20	53	10:5-11	66	25:6-9	16, 20
1:21-23	19	10:5-54	73	25:7	57, 95
2	52	10:12	73	25:8	95
2:2	39	10:12-19	66	25:9	102
2:2-4	17, 19, 21, 38, 39, 42,	10:20-21	80	26:5	15
	43, 50, 54, 85, 91	10:22	51	26:9	96
2:3	39, 84	10:28-34	17	26:14, 16, 21	52
2:4	21	11	21, 28, 68	26:19	95
2:6-8	51, 80	11:1-5	17, 65	27:1	57, 97
2:10-18	38	11:2	19, 44	27:11	5, 96
2:11-22	53, 73	11:6-9	19, 21, 53, 93	27:12-13	57
2:12, 17	15	11:9	5	28-33	18, 28, 57
3:1-4:6	43, 54	11:9-10	65	28:1-8	80
4	51	11:10-16	18	28:9-18	80
4:2-6	43	12:1	96	28:16, 21	99
4:4	44, 46, 85	13	14, 17, 61, 66, 73, 77	29:10	94
5:1-7	88	13-21	52	29:11, 13	112
5:2, 4, 7	102	13:1-14:32	29, 51	29:14	97
5:24-25	80	13:11	52	29:18	98
6:1, 3	39	13:12	73	29:22-24	5
6:5	39, 40	13:17-19	31	30	100, 101
6:8-13	40	13:19	66	30:9, 12-18	5
6:9-10	4, 97, 111, 112	14	61, 66, 73	30:18	23
6:11-13	66, 99	14:4b-5, 7	15	32	59
7	33, 98	14:11-15	73	32:1-8	5
7-9	6, 11, 29, 43, 95	14:22-27	67	32:3	98
7-14	57	14:24-27	31	32:15	97
7:1-9	53, 59	14:28-32	33	32:15-20	45
7:2	62, 66	14:29-32	29	32:17-18	93
7:4	9, 99	15-16	33	33:2	102
7:7-9	80	15-22	66, 67	33:14-16	93, 100
7:9	9, 23, 99	15:1-16:14	29	33:22	101
7:9b, 10-14	57	17:1-8	29	34:1-10	53
7:11	23	17:4-11	80	34:5-15	28
7:14	16, 17, 112, 114, 115	18	68	34:14-15	21
7:14-16	63	18-19	29, 59, 67	34:16	45
7:17	65	19	18, 68	34:17	6
7:17-8:8	62, 65	19:12-17	67	35:5	98
7:17-10:25	28	19:18-28	68	35:5-6	114
8:5-19	31	20	68	36-37	42, 69
8:9-22	66	21	18, 61, 73	36-39	11, 18, 57, 68
8:17	16, 99, 102	21:1	52	36:10	68
8:23-9:1	112	21:1-10	29, 51	37:7, 36	69
9	21, 28	21:11-12	33	37:20	6
9:1	80	21:11-17	29	38	69
9:1-6	114, 115	22	28, 51, 57, 68	38:19	95
9:1-10:34	54	22:3-4	80	39	61, 69
9:5[6]	63	23-27	52, 57	39:6-7	69
9:6-7	17, 63	23:1-18	29	40	43, 80, 88, 95
9:8-21	80	23:17	52	40-44	15
9:8-10:4	66	24	33	40-48	24, 33, 35, 51
9:8-10:19	28	24-25	20, 95	40-66	34, 69